Ready for

B2 First
for Schools

Ready for B2 First for Schools

Editorial Manager: Simona Franzoni
Editorial department: Sabina Cedraro, Simona Pisauri
Art Director: Marco Mercatali
Page layout: Tecnostampa
Picture Editor: Giorgia D'Angelo
Production Manager: Francesco Capitano
Cover design: Curvilinee

© 2021 ELI S.r.l
P.O. Box 6
62019 Recanati
Italy
info@elionline.com
www.elionline.com

Acknowledgements
Photos: Shutterstock

First reprint January 2023

Printed in Italy by Tecnostampa – Pigini Group Printing Division
Loreto – Trevi 21.83.122.1
ISBN: 978-88-536-3298-2

Contents

B2 First for Schools

The updated **B2 First for Schools** exam (for exam sessions from January 2015) is made up of four papers developed to test students' English language skills. It shows that a student has the language skills they need to communicate in an English-speaking environment.

Reading and Use of English   1 hour 15 minutes

Part & Task Type	Format	Number of questions
1 Multiple-choice cloze	A cloze test containing 8 gaps and followed by four-option multiple-choice items	8
2 Open Cloze	A cloze text containing 8 gaps	8
3 Word formation	A text containing 8 gaps. Each gap corresponds to a word. The stems of the missing words are given beside the text and must be changed to form the missing word.	8
4 Key word transformations	Six separate items, each with a lead-in sentence and a gapped second sentence to be completed in two to five words, one of which is a given 'key word'.	6
5 Multiple choice	A text followed by 6 four-option multiple-choice questions.	6
6 Gapped text	A text from which sentences have been removed and placed in jumbled order after the text. Candidates must decide from where in the text the sentences have been removed	6
7 Multiple matching	A text or several short texts preceded by multiple-matching questions. Candidates must match prompts to elements in the text.	10

Writing   1 hour 20 minutes

Part & Task Type	Format	Number of tasks
1 Essay	Candidates are required to write an essay giving their opinion on the essay title using the ideas given and providing an idea of their own.	1 (compulsory)
2 From the following: article, email / letter, sport, review	Candidates have a choice of task. In questions 2-4, the tasks provide candidates with a clear context, topic, purpose and target reader for their writing.	3 (choose one)

Listening   40 minutes

Part & Task Type	Format	Number of questions
1 Multiple choice	Eight short unrelated extracts, of approximately 30 seconds each, from monologues or exchanges between interacting speakers. There is one multiple-choice question per extract, each with three options.	8
2 Sentence completion	A monologue lasting approximately 3-4 minutes. Candidates are required to complete the sentences with information heard on the recording.	10
3 Multiple matching	Five short related monologues, of approximately 30 seconds each. The five multiple-matching questions require selection of the correct option from a list of eight.	5
4 Multiple choice	An interview or an exchange between two speakers lasting approximately 3-4 minutes. There are seven multiple-choice questions, each with three options.	7

Speaking   14 minutes

Part & Task Type	Format	Time
1 Personal questions	General interactional and social language.	2 minutes
2 Talking about photos	Organising a larger unit of discourse; comparing, describing, expressing opinions.	4 minutes
3 Collaborative tasks	Sustaining an interaction, exchanging ideas, expressing and justifying opinions, agreeing and / or disagreeing, suggesting, speculating, evaluating, reaching a decision through negotiation, etc.	4 minutes
4 Further discussion	Expressing and justifying opinions, agreeing and / or disagreeing.	4 minutes

Paper 1

Part 1, page 12
Multiple-choice cloze
In **Part One** it is important to think about both the meaning and the grammar of the word as well as collocations, for example:

2 The adverb missing here must be one that form a collocation with the conjunction 'than'.
2 The preposition missing here must be one that forms a common phrasal verb.

Part 2, page 13
Open cloze
In **Part Two** you need to think about the grammar of the sentence and look out for missing auxiliary verbs, prepositions, relative pronouns, linking words etc., for example:

10 This gap clearly needs a relative pronoun: which one?
16 You have to fill in this gap with a reflexive pronoun: which one?

Part 3, page 14
Word formation
In **Part Three** you should always identify the part of speech which is missing (is it a noun, an adjective, an adverb or a verb?). If it's a noun, think about whether it should be in the singular or plural and if there is a negative form, which fits better than the positive. What prefix can you add? If it's an adjective or adverb think if it should be positive or negative and which prefix you can add to make it negative. If it's a verb think about the subject it agrees with; is it singular or plural? Think about what it follows; should it be a gerund or infinitive? Finally what tense should it be in? For example:

18 Here you need a noun. What is the noun referred to the verb 'inhabit'?
23 Here you need a word which follows a verb. What can it be: an adjective or an adverb?

Part 4, page 15
Key word transformations
The most important thing to remember in **Part Four** is to follow the instructions; do NOT change the word given and only use between 2 and 5 words. Try to keep the second sentence as similar as possible to the first one and be as consistent as possible with verb tenses. For example:

25 What follows the verb 'offer': a gerund or an infinitive whit 'to'?
27 What happens to a verb when you use 'although' instead of 'despite'?
28 What expression with 'time' means the same as 'not late'?

Paper 1

Part 5, pages 16-17
Multiple choice

In **Part Five** you are being tested on your general understanding of the text and some of the specific detailed information it includes. You are also being tested on your skills of working out the meaning of words and phrases from the context as well as how well you understand referencing; that is using words like 'it' and 'that' to refer to people or things. With multiple-choice questions it is important to read the whole answer and not only look at individual words. Identify the part of the text which gives you the answer and underline it. Think about synonyms for words in the text and ways to explain the same information in different words. Finally remember there are often distractor answers which may contain words from the text but incorrect information, for example, sometimes the answers say the opposite to the text but contain some of the same words.

31 The key to the answer is in the second paragraph. What are the key words and expressions here? Underline them.
36 What is the key sentence to answer question 36 in the last paragraph?

Part 6, pages 18-19
Gapped text

In **Part Six** you are being tested on how well you understand the flow of a text and referencing; that is referring to people and things using words like 'it' and 'they'. You need to look carefully at the sentences before and after the gap for clues as well as think about the sense of the whole paragraph. When you have chosen the sentence which you think best fits each space, always read through the whole paragraph to make sure it makes sense. For example:

37 Which could be the possible subject in the missing sentence?
38 What can be found below the surface of the sea?
41 What do you call a ship used to tranport goods?

Part 7, pages 20-21
Multiple matching

For **Part Seven** you need to use scanning skills. Read all the texts quickly to begin with so you know what each is about then read the questions and underline key words. To find the correct answer scan the texts for the information you have underlined in the questions. When you find the information underline it so you will be able to check it again easily. Look for synonyms and expressions which have a similar meaning to the words used in the question. Remember in this part the information is somewhere in the text; that is, it is not true or false or multiple choice, you simply have to find it. For example:

43 The key word here is 'setback'. Search for any reference to a problem in the texts.
46 Here you should search for references to metals in the texts.
52 The word you could search for in the texts here would probably be the name of an award.

Paper 2

Part 1, page 22
Question 1: writing an essay
1 Guidance:

- Begin your essay by referring to the general topic and the first question.
- Include all the indicated notes.
- Use simple and short sentences and read them again to check they're correct.
- Be sure you have expressed your own idea.
- Check your work for accuracy, punctuation and spelling.

Part 2, page 23
Question 2: writing an article, a letter/email, a report, a review, a story, a set text ('First for Schools' only)
2 Guidance:

- Stick to the question, avoid simply outlining the plot.
- Show the examiner that you know the film well.
- Don't attempt to answer the question if you are asked a question about the film that you hadn't considered before.
- Check your work for accuracy, punctuation and spelling.

3 Guidance:

- Begin with some basic information about your town. Include some geographical features.
- Include all the specific information required.
- Give your recommendation for places of interest.
- Check your work for accuracy, punctuation and spelling.

Paper 2

4 Guidance:
- Express your reaction to the news.
- Answer Sam's question, making sure you cover all the points.
- Include interesting and useful descriptions and explanations.
- Tell something about your own experience.
- Suggest visiting some useful websites.
- Check your work for accuracy, punctuation and spelling.

Paper 3

Part 1, page 24
Multiple choice
- Read and listen to each question carefully.
- Highlight the key words in the situation/question and think about what you might hear.
- After each question decide your answer before looking at the options.
- Pay attention to negatives and conditionals which may try to mislead you.
- Use the second listening to check your answer.

For example:

2 Search for something which expresses surprise in the parent's reaction.

6 Search for something which describes one of the three adjectives in the options.

Part 2, page 25
Sentence completion
The questions are answered in order in the listening text.
- Make sure what you write fits the space grammatically.
- Although marks are not deducted for spelling, try to spell the words correctly.
- While you are waiting for the listening, begin to look at the spaces and predict what kind of information is needed in the space: is it a number, an adjective, a verb, etc.?
- You will hear the piece twice. After the first time, study the questions you haven't managed to answer. What did you hear which might go in the spaces?
- When you have finished, check your answers. Do they make sense, or are they obviously wrong?

Part 3, page 26
Multiple matching
- Read the instructions carefully to find out what topic the speakers will be talking about.
- Read the topics A-H and try to predict ideas or words you expect to hear.
- In the first listening decide on your answers.
- Use the second listening to check your answers.
- Remember that if one answer is wrong, it could mean that most of the other answers are in the wrong place.
- Remember that this part can be confusing because sometimes a word in one option may appear in more than one extract. You need to focus on the differences between the speakers.

Part 4, page 27
Multiple choice
- Read the instructions carefully to find out what topic the speakers will be talking about.
- Before you listen, read the topic sentences and try to predict ideas or words you expect to hear.
- Use the first listening to decide on your answers.
- Use the second listening to check your answers.

For example:

25 The key word here is spacecraft. Concentrate on that.

27 The word 'marsquakes' is similar to another word. Which one?

Paper 4

Part 1, page 28
Conversation
- Answer the questions as fully as you can; do not only reply 'yes' or 'no' but explain why and give examples where appropriate.
- Always answer the question the examiner asks you. If you don't understand ask them to repeat it.
- Do not give pre-prepared answers.

Part 2, pages 29-31
Individual 'long turn'
- Make sure you answer the question and, if possible, use the words on the paper in your answer and make sure you explain **why** these people have chosen the places shown in the photos. *'I think these people have chosen these places...'*
- Make sure you continue to speak for the full minute. You will lose marks if you finish too soon.
- Make sure you **compare** the photos and do not talk about them individually.
- Use linking expressions, for example, *both photos show... however, while, whereas...*

Part 3, pages 32-33
Two-way conversation
In this part it is very important that you have a discussion with your partner and interact together.
- Ask your partner what they think and always try to respond to what they say.
- Use expressions like *I agree, you're right, that's true or I don't agree with you, perhaps, but...*
- Make sure you talk for the full 3 minutes.
- Make sure you move the conversation on to include as many of the pictures as possible and make some conclusions during your discussion.

Part 4, pages 32-33
Discussion
In this part you will be asked your opinion about the topic you discussed in Part 3.
- Like with **Part 1** make sure you answer the question you are asked and give full answers.
- Explain why you think something and give examples where appropriate.
- If you don't understand ask the examiner to repeat the question.
- If you don't know what to say use fillers like *well, that's a difficult question* to give yourself time to think.
- Try not to answer by saying *I don't know*.

Part 1

For questions **1-8**, read the text below and decide which answer (**A**, **B**, **C** or **D**) best fits each gap. There is an example at the beginning (**0**).

Mark your answers **on the separate answer sheet.**

Example:

| 0 | **A** how | **B** when | **C** where | **D** why |

0	A	B	C	D
	—	▬	—	—

Super Thursday

The first Thursday in October is (**0**) _____ publishers release the largest number of books in the year. It is now called Super Thursday. This year more than 500 books will (**1**) _____ on the shelves of booksellers. Most of these are the more expensive hardbacks (**2**) _____ than paperbacks or books that can be read on e-readers.

The strength of the sales of hardbacks has (**3**) _____ many people in publishing. A few years ago, people predicted that e-books would become much more popular than paper books. They were (**4**) _____ to produce, more environmentally friendly and readers could easily (**5**) _____ hundreds of titles on an electronic device.

Although the number of people owning e-books continues to rise, sales of hardbacks have also gone (**6**) _____. They account for about 20% of the overall book market. According to Philip Jones, the editor of the magazine *The Bookseller*, there are several (**7**) _____ for this: a hardback is a mark of quality and shows that a publisher really believes in the title. They also stand out when on (**8**) _____ in a bookshop.

1	**A** apply	**B** appear	**C** approach	**D** appeal
2	**A** other	**B** of	**C** for	**D** rather
3	**A** despised	**B** surprised	**C** surpassed	**D** inspired
4	**A** cheaper	**B** higher	**C** longer	**D** wider
5	**A** shop	**B** make	**C** lose	**D** store
6	**A** up	**B** on	**C** in	**D** by
7	**A** concepts	**B** returns	**C** revisions	**D** reasons
8	**A** replay	**B** display	**C** request	**D** balance

Part 2

For questions **9-16**, read the text below and think of the word that best fits each gap. Use only **one** word in each gap. There is an example at the beginning (**0**).

Write your answers **IN CAPITAL LETTERS on the separate answer sheet.**

Example: | 0 | | O | F | | | | | | | | | | | | | | | | | |

Wes Anderson's Films

One of the unusual films in the list (**0**) _____ box office hits is *Isle of Dogs*, directed by Wes Anderson.
He is known for making films that are very visual but (**9**) _____ have interesting but uncomplicated stories. My favourite is *The Grand Budapest Hotel*, which follows the extraordinary adventures of guests and staff (**10**) _____ occupy the hotel in the 1930s.

In contrast, the *Isle of Dogs* is made (**11**) _____ stop motion. This is an animated technique (**12**) _____ objects are moved in very small steps and
(**13**) _____ photographed. When the frames are played back
(**14**) _____ fast speed the objects appear to move independently. The director also used it with great success in his previous film, *Fantastic Mr. Fox*, based (**15**) _____ the children's story by Roald Dahl.
Isle of Dogs is set in Japan in the near future. After an outbreak of dog fever, all the canines in Megasaki City are sent away to Trash Island where they have to look after (**16**) _____ .

Part 3

For questions **17-24** read the text below. Use the word given in capitals at the end of some of the lines to form a word that fits in the gap **in the same line**. There is an example at the beginning (**0**).

Write your answers **IN CAPITAL LETTERS on the separate answer sheet.**

Example: | 0 | A | P | P | R | O | X | I | M | A | T | E | L | Y | | | | | | |

Easter Island

Easter Island is in the Pacific Ocean (**0**) _____ 4,000 kilometres off the coast of Chile. It was given its European name because Dutch (**17**) _____ landed there on Easter Day in 1772. They were extremely surprised by what they found. There were hundreds of huge stone statues, called *moai* that had apparently been built by the (**18**) _____ .

APPROXIMATE

EXPLORE

INHABIT

The *moai* are over 4 metres tall and were probably made to honour the chiefs and other (**19**) _____ people. The people who constructed them belonged to a Polynesian culture called *Rapa Nui*. They travelled from (**20**) _____ islands in the Pacific Ocean and developed a distinct (**21**) _____ and artistic culture from the tenth to the (**22**) _____ century. During this period, there were probably over 12,000 people there.

IMPORTANCE

DISTANCE
ARCHITECTURE
SIXTEEN

After this date, the population decreased (**23**) _____ . There are a number of theories suggesting what happened. Until fairly recently, the most convincing idea was that the (**24**) _____ cut down the trees, possibly to use for building, and in the process destroyed the ecosystem.

DRAMA

ISLAND

Part 4

For questions **25-30**, complete the second sentence so that it has a similar meaning to the first sentence, using the word given. **Do not change the word given.** You must use between **two** and **five** words, including the word given. Here is an example (**0**).

Example:

0   Only a few people saw those beautiful birds.
   SEEN
   The beautiful birds _____ a few people.

The gap can be filled by the words 'Were seen by only', so you write:

Example: |0| |W|E|R|E| |S|E|E|N| |B|Y| |O|N|L|Y| | |

Write **only** the missing words **IN CAPITAL LETTERS on the separate answer sheet**.

25   'I can give you a lift to the station,' my sister said to me.
   OFFERED
   My sister _____ a lift to the station.

26   We haven't been to this museum for ages.
   SINCE
   _____ we've been to this museum.

27   Jane still went to school, despite not feeling very well.
   ALTHOUGH
   Jane still went to school, _____ very well.

28   Their plane isn't going to be late when it lands at Heathrow Airport.
   TIME
   Their plane is going to land _____.

29   We are very lucky to have such a lot of good friends.
   SO
   We are very lucky to have _____.

30   Do you think the government really wants to cut taxes?
   FAVOUR
   Do you think the government really _____ taxes?

Part 5

You are going to read an extract from a guidebook to London in which Debbie Dodie writes about a well-known shopping destination. For questions **31-36**, choose the answer (**A, B, C** or **D**) which you think fits best according to the text.

Mark your answers **on the separate answer sheet**.

A Famous Department Store

Harrods is a name that is familiar to many tourists but surprisingly few people know much about it. Now you can find out. It is a large department store in Knightsbridge, an area in the centre of London. The
5 store has a long history. The founder, Charles Henry Harrod, was born in 1799 in a small town by the sea, which in those days seemed a long way from the capital city. His father was not well off and Charles Henry had to go to work to increase the family's
10 income.

He started out selling tea and groceries in a little shop in London's East End. His early career suffered a major setback when he was arrested for selling goods that had been stolen. He spent a year in
15 prison. When he was released in 1837, he went back to what he had been doing. The business started to expand and he moved the shop premises to a street close to where the store is today. Charles worked very hard and was successful but grew tired after
20 being there for over twenty-five years and handed over the company to his son.
Charles Digby was much more energetic and innovative than his more careful father. However, in 1883, another disaster struck. Just before Christmas,
25 the shop burnt to the ground. Many people believed that this would be the end of Harrods, but Charles Digby thought otherwise.
He immediately rented somewhere else and delivered all the orders he had promised his customers. His
30 reputation increased and the business became even more successful. At the end of the century, Charles Digby decided to retire. Although he had eight children, none of them wanted to take over and the business was sold.

35 Today, the store has 330 departments and 23 restaurants which serve a wide range of food, including afternoon tea, which can be enjoyed in the Tea Rooms. It has become a tradition for many of the long-standing customers to escape there after a hard
40 day's shopping. The meal consists of a number of

delicious sandwiches and cakes served on trays with a choice of either Indian or Chinese tea. Despite the high cost, there are long queues of people every day. I, for one, am always prepared to wait to sample the delights.   45
Throughout its long history, Harrods has had an influence on how people dress, what they eat and the way they furnish their homes. However, one of its major innovations was the introduction of moving staircases. The first escalator was introduced in   50
1898. Many customers were initially terrified of using them and because of that the brave ones who attempted the journey, were given a glass of brandy to steady their nerves when they reached the top.

Another surprising thing about the store is that it   55
used to have a pet department. It opened in 1917 and you could buy not only domestic pets but wild animals such as lions, tigers and panthers as well! In fact, the son of the former King of Albania bought an elephant there in 1967 as a gift for then California   60
governor, Ronald Reagan. The department stopped selling exotic pets in 1976 but did not finally close until 2014.
Harrods attracts a large number of people. In theory, anyone can enter. You do not need to   65
be rich or even make a purchase. However, you should be careful about what you wear. In 1989, the management introduced a dress code. People wearing cycling shorts, flip-flops, beach clothes and more surprisingly, uniforms, except police officers,   70
are denied entry. It applies to everyone. Some very famous people have been turned away and told to wear something different if they want to get in.
In the age of online shopping, many large department stores in London are in financial difficulty and find it   75
harder to persuade people not only to come through the doors but also to spend money. Harrods has gone against this trend by offering something that is unique. It has managed to keep the style that made it successful in the past and still satisfy the needs of   80
today's demanding and diverse shoppers.

31 According to the text what do we know about the life of Charles Henry Harrod?
  A He was born in a large house in central London.
  B He had a criminal record because he was fraudulent.
  C He inherited a large sum of money from his family.
  D He was forced to hand over the business to his son.

32 Charles Digby Harrod decided to sell up in order
  A to make sure his children could continue to work there.
  B to open up another store in a different part of London.
  C to allow another company to run the store.
  D to pay for the damage that was caused by the fire.

33 What is the writer's opinion about having afternoon tea in Harrods?
  A It is not worth waiting in a long queue to enjoy it.
  B It is a recent innovation that will not attract many customers.
  C It is too expensive as the food and beverage menu is very limited.
  D It is a good place to relax when you are shopping in the store.

34 Shoppers may be stopped from going into the front entrance of Harrods because
  A they are dressed in clothes that are not appropriate.
  B they are celebrities who have a special way to get in.
  C they haven't got enough money to buy anything.
  D they don't know the correct password for the door.

35 In 'because of that' in line 52 'that' refers to the fact that
  A most shoppers looked forward to using the escalators.
  B the escalators were a common sight in many London stores.
  C the management only wanted a few people to shop on the higher floors.
  D the experience of going on an escalator was a challenge for shoppers.

36 What is the writer's opinion about Harrods in the last paragraph?
  A She believes it hasn't changed with the times.
  B She thinks it is now less fashionable than it was.
  C She predicts that it will not meet the future demands of its customers.
  D She feels it has adapted well to the changes in the market.

Part 6

You are going to read a newspaper article about a project in the Black Sea. Six sentences have been removed from the article. Choose from the sentences **A-G** the one which fits each gap (**37-42**). There is one extra sentence which you do not need to use.

Mark your answers **on the separate answer sheet**.

A Ship at the Bottom of the Sea

A team of archaeologists, marine specialists and scientists have been working on the Black Sea Maritime Archaeological Project (MAP). [37] During their research, they have found over sixty shipwrecks – ships which have sunk and remained on the seabed – in the Black Sea over the past three years.

[38] It was found below the surface of the Black Sea off the coast of Bulgaria. When the team of scientists discovered it, they used two underwater robotic explorers to make a 3-D image of the ship and extract a piece of wood which they sent to the University of Southampton, UK to be carbon-dated. The carbon-dating showed that the ship has been there for about two and a half thousand years. This makes it the oldest known discovery of its kind. Ships usually break up when they sink to the bottom of the sea. [39] It has been lying on the ocean bed about two kilometres from the surface.

There is little or no oxygen beyond one hundred and fifty metres down due to a thick covering of salt water over fresh water. At this depth, without oxygen, organic material such as wood stays in good condition, due to unique chemical elements in the water, so parts of the ship's construction, such as the mast, can be clearly identified.

[40] During the three-year project, remote-controlled deep-water camera systems have been used to film the ship to take photographs and measurements. Complete fish bones have been seen on it, showing what people used to eat and there is some rope which has remained in the position it was in when the boat sank.

It is thought that it was a Greek trading ship, used to transport goods to Greek colonies on the Black Sea coast. [41] If this is the case, the ship possibly contains gold, wine, oil or other precious metals. As it is so deep, the team will need specialist diving equipment before they can return to explore the ship to look for its cargo. [42] This gives a clear illustration of what the ship in the Black Sea would have looked like. The vase, currently on display in the British Museum, is dated 480 BC.

Scientists are very excited by the find because they know this will give them much more information on ship-building and sailing in the ancient world. They are interested in what it can tell them about technology, trade and shipping movements in that area.

A   The cargo it was carrying could still be inside.

B   However, this one is in extremely good condition and completely intact.

C   They have been exploring the sea to examine prehistoric changes in sea levels.

D   Ancient Roman ships have also been found in this area.

E   It also means that it is too deep for people to dive to the shipwreck.

F   A picture of a similar ship appears on a Greek vase called the *Siren Vase*.

G   A 23-metre ship has recently been discovered by the team.

Part 7

You are going to read part of an article about Bob Dylan. For questions **43-52**, choose from the sections (**A-D**). The sections may be chosen more than once.

Mark your answers **on the separate answer sheet**.

In which section does the writer mention

when Dylan suffers a setback?	43	
Dylan's artwork depicting unusual people?	44	
the reason why Dylan altered his work?	45	
what he created out of metal?	46	
how he began his artistic career?	47	
what his age is?	48	
Dylan's commercial success as an artist?	49	
paintings done when he was on tour?	50	
an exhibition which looks back on his work?	51	
the reason why he won an international award?	52	

Bob Dylan – The Artist

A

Bob Dylan is an internationally renowned singer, songwriter and author. He is held in such high esteem that he won the Nobel Prize in Literature in October 2016 for having created new poetic expressions within the great American song tradition. He is also a prolific artist and painter. He started by doing drawings for his album covers in the 1960s and in 1974 spent two intensive months studying painting. A book of 92 drawings called *Drawn Blank* was published in 1994. One of his major exhibitions called *Bob Dylan on Canvas* was at the Halcyon Gallery in central London. The show opened in October 2008 and it was the first time that Dylan displayed works he had painted using acrylics. The paintings quickly sold out and this inspired him into a burst of creativity using this medium.

C

His extraordinary creative energy did not diminish and in February 2013, an exhibition of 23 paintings completed in New Orleans went on display at the Palazzo Reale, Milan. Later in the year, in a change of direction he exhibited work, again at the Halycon Gallery, of gates created from iron and bronze. His work in *Mondo Scripto* features some of his most iconic lyrics which are handwritten by him on pen and paper and accompanied by an original pencil drawing. In this way he has fused together a number of his artistic disciplines. He has changed some of the words in his songs and even completely rewritten one, especially for the exhibition, in order to bring a new perspective to his writing.

B

He completed 50 paintings which became known as the *Brazil Series.* These were exhibited at the Statens Museum for Kunst in Copenhagen, Denmark which opened in 2010. Visitors saw how the artist had made preliminary drawings while he was in Brazil with his band. He developed these into richly coloured pictures of what he had seen while he was travelling. These included landscapes of the countryside and cityscapes particularly showing the poorer areas known as *favelas.* There were also paintings of interesting characters such as musicians, card players and even criminals. The next major landmark in his career was his first show in New York in autumn 2011. The *Asia Series* depicted the time he spent in China, Japan, Vietnam and Korea. The following year he was awarded the United States Presidential Medal of Freedom by Barack Obama.

D

Although Dylan is now in his late seventies, he continues to write, paint, draw and give concerts.
His singing voice is not as good as it was when he first played in Greenwich Village as a folk singer.
At a recent concert he was even booed when he left the stage. However, his artwork continues to inspire people from different generations. A recent display of his work in Shanghai, China called *Retrospectrum* aims to tell the story of his art rather than focusing on individual pieces. It is difficult to predict what he will come up with for future projects. Throughout his long career his desire to experiment has produced many surprises.

Part 1

You **must** answer this question. Write your answer in **140-190** words in an appropriate style.

1   In your English class, you have been talking about sustainable tourism. Now, your English teacher has asked you to write an essay.

Write an essay using **all** the notes and giving reasons for your point of view.

Some people say that tourism has a negative effect on the environment. Do you agree?

Notes
Write about:
1 whether sustainable tourism is important
2 an example of sustainable tourism
3 _____ (your own idea)

Part 2

Write an answer to **one** of the questions **2-4** in this part. Write your answer in **140-190** words in an appropriate style.

2   You see this notice in your school English-language magazine.

Film Club Magazine

Have you watched a fictional film recently which had an interesting story?

Write a review of the film. Tell us why the story was interesting and whether you would recommend the film to other people.

The writer of the best review will receive two cinema tickets.

Write your **review**.

3   You see this announcement on an English-speaking website.

Articles about our town

We want to inform tourists about our wonderful town and we welcome your ideas.

To help attract tourists to the town, write about a local place of interest that you think is special.

Name the place of interest.
Say why you think it's special.
Tell them the best time of year to visit.

Write your **article**.

4   You have received this email from your English-speaking friend Sam.

I'm interested in getting a holiday job this summer, but I'm not sure what to do.
As you know me well, can you suggest a job I would be good at? What do you think
I could learn from this job? What's the best way to travel around in my free time?

Write your **email**.

Part 1

(1) You will hear people talking in eight different situations. For questions **1-8**, choose the best answer (**A**, **B** or **C**).

1   You hear two people, who have not met for a while, talking. What do they discuss?
     A   How much they earn.
     B   What they do in their free time.
     C   Why they haven't seen each other.

2   You hear a head teacher's assistant talking to a parent. What is the parent surprised about?
     A   Where her daughter is.
     B   How long the lessons last.
     C   What the head teacher is doing.

3   You hear a conversation between Kevin, an employee at a TV company, and Rebecca, a customer. What does she do during the conversation?
     A   She says she's sorry.
     B   She gets annoyed.
     C   She asks for his phone number.

4   You hear a person who works for a cruise ship company talking. What is he doing?
     A   Criticising young people's behaviour.
     B   Announcing the winners of a competition.
     C   Explaining why changes are being made.

5   You hear a post office worker talking to a customer. During the conversation the customer
     A   gives some information.
     B   asks for advice.
     C   makes an excuse.

6   You hear two people talking about their new neighbour. What is their attitude towards her?
     A   welcoming
     B   indifferent
     C   hostile

7   You hear part of a recorded message. What is the main purpose of the speaker?
     A   to make suggestions
     B   to provide historical information
     C   to give detailed directions

8   You hear a customer and a shop assistant talking. What is the man doing?
     A   giving an apology
     B   describing a product
     C   making a complaint

Part 2

(2) You will hear a man called Elliot talking about extraterrestrial activity. For questions **9-18**, complete the sentences with a word or short phrase.

The Roswell Incident

Elliot believes that extraterrestrial activity is a [9 _____] subject to talk about.

Elliot wants his audience to decide whether the Roswell incident is [10 _____]

The town of Roswell is situated in New Mexico in [11 _____] of the United States.

William Brazel, who discovered the unusual materials, worked on [12 _____]

Elliot says that a nurse was [13 _____] when she went into the hospital room and saw the three bodies.

Immediately after the incident, a government official claimed that what people believed was a flying disk was actually [14 _____]

The newspaper *National Enquirer* finally reported that there might have been a cover-up [15 _____] after the incident took place.

Elliot says that thousands of people visit the site every year even though [16 _____] exists to show what happened.

Scientists have not been able to find any [17 _____] that might have come from an alien landing.

Elliot suggests that the US government might not want [18 _____] to know what happened at Roswell.

Part 3

(3) You will hear five short extracts in which people are talking about their evening at the theatre. For questions **19-23**, choose from the list (**A-H**) what each speaker likes most about his/her evening. Use the letters only once. There are three extra letters which you do not need to use.

A	the way the play was written	Speaker 1	19
B	the age of the actors	Speaker 2	20
C	the length of the play	Speaker 3	21
D	the quality of the acting	Speaker 4	22
E	the incident before the play began	Speaker 5	23
F	the cost of the seats in the theatre		
G	the journey to the theatre		
H	the style of the stage design		

Part 4

(4) You will hear part of a conversation with a woman called Helen and a man called Tom about an event in outer space. For questions **24-30**, choose the best answer (**A**, **B** or **C**).

24   What does Tom first say about the landing on Mars?
    A   It was a story from science fiction.
    B   It made him feel quite sad.
    C   It was an extraordinary feat.

25   What most impressed Tom about the NASA spacecraft?
    A   the quality of its cameras
    B   the reduction in its speed
    C   the way it suddenly disappeared

26   What most interests scientists about the inside of Mars?
    A   its composition
    B   its size
    C   its age

27   What does Tom say about marsquakes?
    A   They are a type of food.
    B   They are a type of movement.
    C   They are a type of weather.

28   Why does Tom think it is important to know about Mars?
    A   To help solve problems on Earth.
    B   To enable people to inhabit it.
    C   To find out more about how the planets in the solar system developed.

29   What does Tom say about the NASA scientists' behaviour when the spacecraft InSight landed?
    A   They didn't display much emotion.
    B   They expressed delight in their achievements.
    C   They didn't believe it had happened.

30   What is Tom's opinion about the involvement of other countries in the Mars mission?
    A   He thinks it will cause international conflict.
    B   He thinks it will have little scientific benefit.
    C   He thinks it will assist scientific advancement.

Part 1
2 minutes (3 minutes for groups of three)

Good morning/afternoon/evening. My name is ——————— and this is my colleague ———————.

And your names are?

Can I have your mark sheets, please?

Thank you.

First of all we'd like to know something about you.

- Where are you from, (*Candidate A*)?
- And you, (*Candidate B*)?
- What do you like about living (here / name of candidate's home town)?
- And what about you, (*Candidate A/B*)?

Select one or more questions from any of the following categories, as appropriate.

Your family

- Do you live alone or do you live with your family?
- Do you come from a large family or from a small family?
- Does the rest of your family relations live in the same town as yours?
- What do your parents do?
- What's the best thing you like doing with your family?

Shopping

- Where do you usually go shopping?
- How often do you shop online?
- Do you think shopping online is safe? Why? / Why not?
- Tell us about something you've just bought.
- Do you prefer to go shopping alone or with your friends?

Entertainment

- What do you like doing at weekends?
- How often do you watch TV? What's your favourite TV series?
- Do you prefer listening to music at home or going to concerts? Why?
- Do you play any games online? How often do you play them?
- How many books do you read in a year? Would you like to read more?

<table>
<tr><td>

1 Places to live in
2 Families doing things together
</td><td>

Part 2
4 minutes (6 minutes for groups of three)
</td></tr>
</table>

Interlocutor In this part of the test, I'm going to give each of you two photographs. I'd like you to talk about your photographs on your own for about a minute, and also to answer a question about your partner's photographs.

(*Candidate A*), it's your turn first. Here are your photographs. They show **places to live in.**

*Place **Photo 1** in front of Candidate A.*

I'd like you to compare the photographs, and say **what advantages and disadvantages there could be if you lived in these places**.

All right?

Candidate A
⏱ *1 minute*
_____

Interlocutor Thank you.

(*Candidate B*), **would you like to live on a tropical island?**

Candidate B
⏱ *approximately 30 seconds*
_____

Interlocutor Thank you.

Now, (*Candidate B*), here are your photographs; they show **families doing things together.**

*Place **Photo 2** in front of Candidate B.*

I'd like you to compare the photographs, and say **why you think it is important for the families to do these activities togheter**.

All right?

Candidate B
⏱ *1 minute*
_____

Interlocutor Thank you.

(*Candidate A*), **what kind of activities do you usually do with your family?**

Candidate A
⏱ *approximately 30 seconds*
_____

Interlocutor Thank you.

1 (*Candidate A*)

What are the advantages and disadvantages of living in these places?

1

2 (*Candidate B*)

Why do you think it is important for families to do these activities together?

2

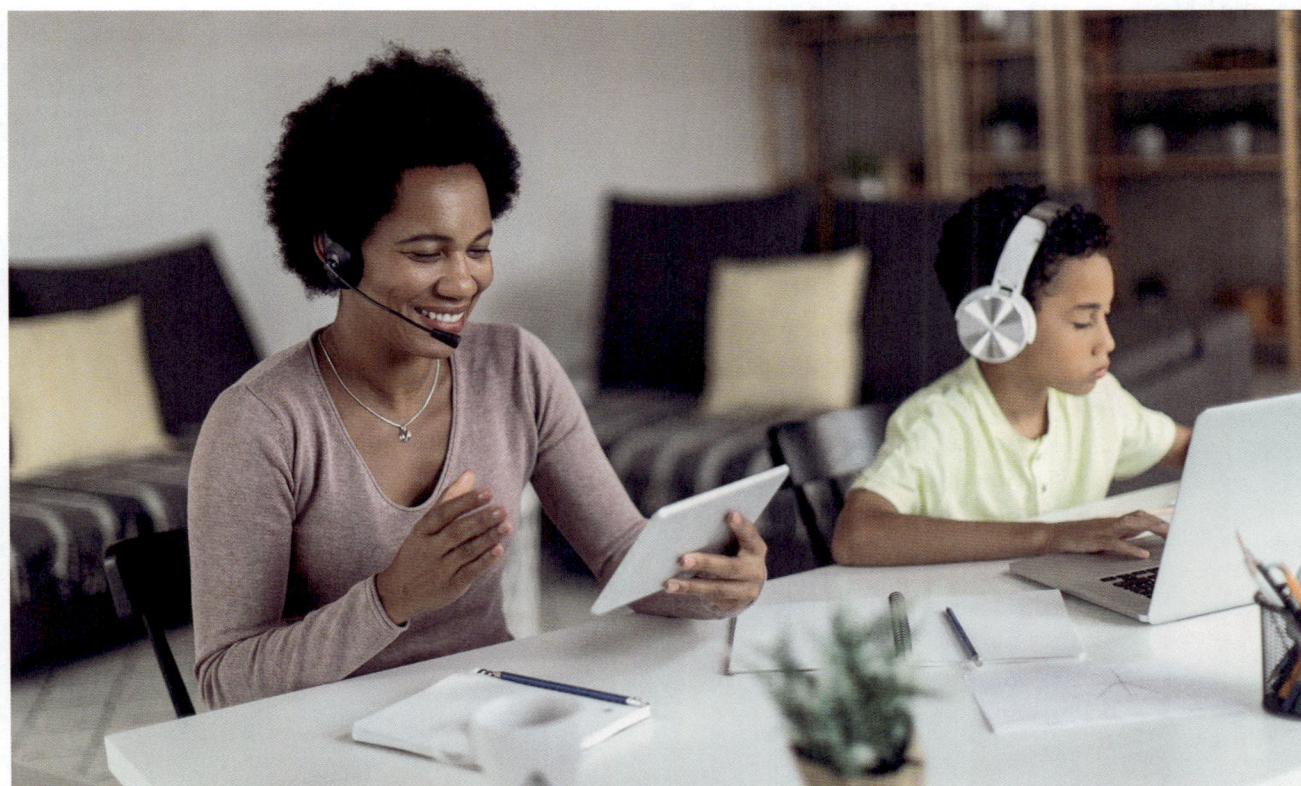

21 Improve school conditions	**Part 3** 4 minutes (5 minutes for groups of three)
	Part 4 4 minutes (6 minutes for groups of three)

Part 3

Interlocutor   Now, I'd like you to talk about something together for about two minutes
(*3 minutes for groups of three*).

**Imagine your school's debate group has decided to do something to improve school
life conditions.** Here are some of the suggestions for what the group can do and a
question for you to discuss. First you have some time to look at the task.

(*The Interlocutor will show the candidates the page with **Task 21** and will allow
15 seconds.*)

Now, talk to each other about **how these activities might improve school life
conditions.**

Candidates
⏱ *2 minutes*
*(3 minutes for
groups of three)*

Interlocutor   Thank you. Now you have about a minute to decide **which two would be the most
effective.**

Candidates
⏱ *1 minute*
*(for pairs and
groups of three)*

Interlocutor   Thank you.

Part 4

Interlocutor   Use the following questions, in order, as appropriate:

- **How important is it to go to a school with good facilities?**
- **Do you think digital learning can improve students' lives? How?**
- **Do you think computers will replace teachers in the future?**
- **Do you think it is important to do sport while at school?**
- **How important is it to go on school trips?**
- **Do you think that going to university will help you find a good job?**

Thank you. That is the end of the test.

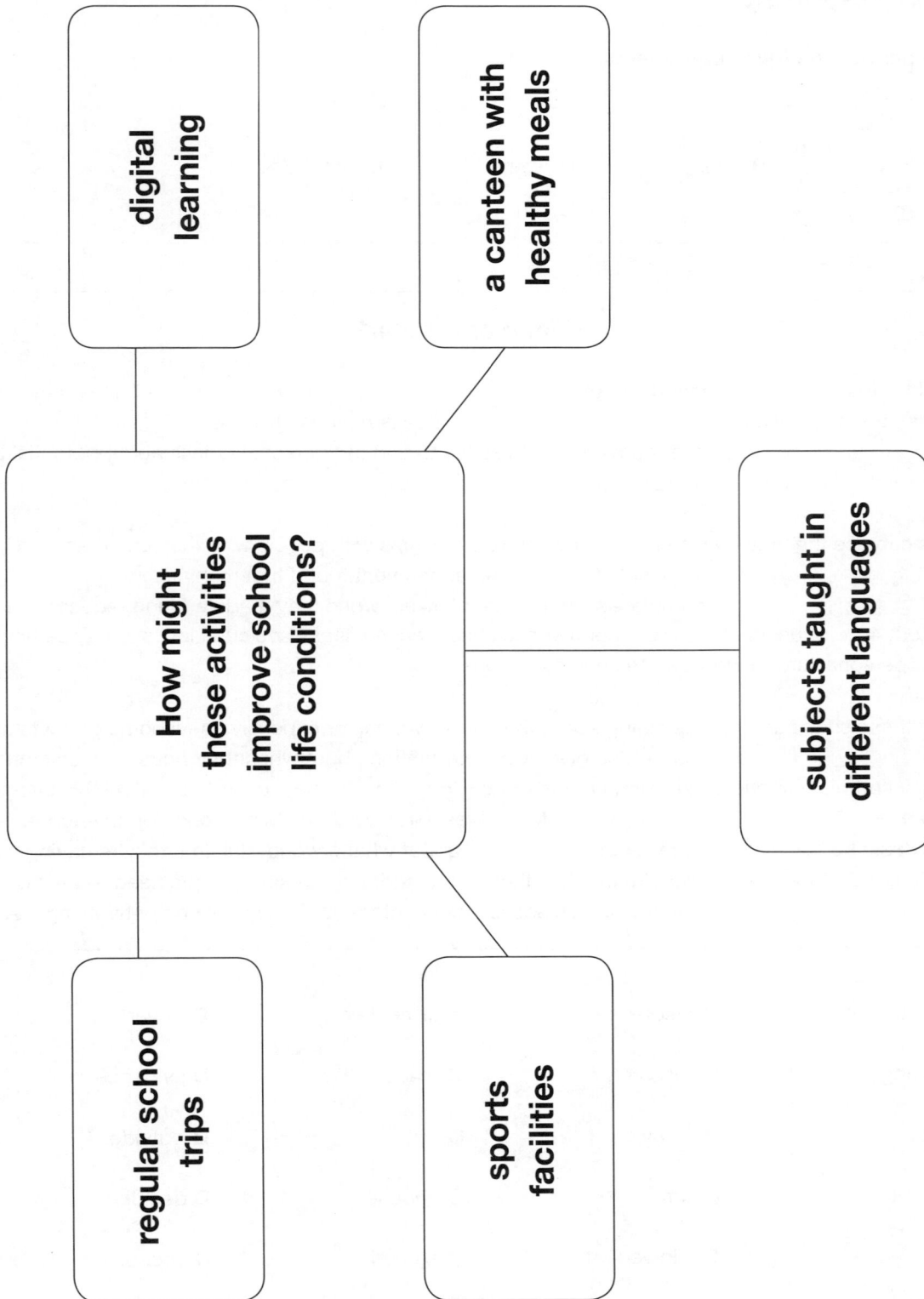

Task 21

digital
learning

a canteen with
healthy meals

**How might
these activities
improve school
life conditions?**

subjects taught in
different languages

regular school
trips

sports
facilities

Part 1

For questions **1-8**, read the text below and decide which answer (**A**, **B**, **C** or **D**) best fits each gap. There is an example at the beginning (**0**).

Mark your answers **on the separate answer sheet.**

Example:

| 0 | **A** sites | **B** places | **C** webs | **D** locations |

0	A	B	C	D
			▬	▭

Friend or burglar?

Users of well-known social networking (**0**) _____ have been warned they may have to pay more for their house (**1**) _____. This is because there is (**2**) _____ that burglars use the sites to find out personal details about potential targets and information like when people will be (**3**) _____ on holiday.

Burglars can use the networking sites to develop relationships with people who they can then (**4**) _____ as people to burgle. An experiment found that many users (**5**) _____ complete strangers as followers when they made a friend request. Also, about 40% of users of the most popular social networking sites have such low security settings that their personal information can be seen by anyone.

Users of these sites can't help boasting about their holiday plans or expensive new home gadgets they've (**6**) _____. Users also give away information about when their house will be empty when they complain about working long hours or how long their journey to work takes. All this information makes life very (**7**) _____ for thieves. Graham Jones who works for an Internet security company said he has seen people sending messages about what a wonderful time they're having on holiday in the Caribbean on a website that has their home address. He says people need to be more (**8**) _____ of just who has access to the information they post on networking websites.

1	**A** assurance	**B** insurance	**C** protection	**D** cover
2	**A** findings	**B** research	**C** clues	**D** evidence
3	**A** gone	**B** away	**C** out	**D** outside
4	**A** target	**B** aim	**C** choose	**D** decide
5	**A** let	**B** allowed	**C** agreed	**D** accepted
6	**A** purchased	**B** found	**C** used	**D** sold
7	**A** difficult	**B** clear	**C** good	**D** easy
8	**A** know	**B** aware	**C** willing	**D** open

Part 2

For questions **9-16**, read the text below and think of the word that best fits each gap. Use only one word in each gap. There is an example at the beginning (**0**).

Write your answers **IN CAPITAL LETTERS on the separate answer sheet.**

Example: | 0 | | I | N | T | O | | | | | | | | | | | | | | |

Recycling

Recycling involves taking used materials and turning them (**0**) _____ new products. It is not a new concept; people have been recycling for hundreds of years but (**9**) _____ rising energy costs since the 1970s it has become more of a necessity and is now common practice. The idea of recycling is (**10**) _____ prevent waste and reduce the consumption of new fresh raw materials.

The (**11**) _____ common materials which are recycled are paper and glass. Some plastics, metals and textiles can also be recycled as well as some electronic equipment. It is now typical to separate household waste into materials (**12**) _____ can and can't be recycled. Recycling points (**13**) _____ glass, paper etc. can be taken to are now common sights in many major towns and cities.

In theory recycling seems obvious; however, in practice it is (**14**) _____ always cost-effective. Often the cost of collection and transportation is greater (**15**) _____ the cost of the energy saved. It also means there are fewer jobs available in industries (**16**) _____ as mining, as demand for raw materials is lower. As a result, recycling is a controversial topic. However, with more government legislation and more incentives being introduced, recycling is clearly on the increase.

Part 3

For questions **17-24** read the text below. Use the word given in capitals at the end of some of the lines to form a word that fits in the gap **in the same line**. There is an example at the beginning (**0**).

Write your answers **IN CAPITAL LETTERS on the separate answer sheet**.

Example: | 0 | | A | C | C | O | U | N | T | A | N | T | | | | | | | | |

Advertising for work

An out of work (**0**) _____ was seen advertising his services   **ACCOUNT**
on a placard outside a busy London station last week. This
(**17**) _____ tactic is reminiscent of scenes from New York's   **USUAL**
Wall Street during the great (**18**) _____ of the 1930s. Daniel   **DEPRESS**
Bell decided to try this drastic approach after months of looking for a job using
more (**19**) _____ methods. He said he had sent out hundreds   **TRADITION**
of CVs and applied to over 70 different jobs but only had five interviews, none of
which were successful.
Now he says he has nothing to lose and hopes to impress prospective
(**20**) _____ with his initiative.   **EMPLOY**

He plans to stand outside the station with his sign during the rush hour and gives
out business cards for as long as it takes to get a job. After just two days he has
received three (**21**) _____ to attend interviews so the plan   **INVITE**
seems to be working. He admits, however, that his (**22**) _____   **PRESENT**
has received mixed (**23**) _____. 'Most people seem   **REACT**
embarrassed and try to look the other way, while others
(**24**) _____ think I am being ridiculous and more than one   **CLEAR**
person openly pointed and laughed at me. I don't care though,' he says, 'they
might find themselves being made redundant by the end of the month. It feels
good to be doing something positive.'

Part 4

For questions **25-30**, complete the second sentence so that it has a similar meaning to the first sentence, using the word given. **Do not change the word given.** You must use between **two** and **five** words, includin the word given. Here is an example (**0**).

Example:

0   I haven't seen him for at least 2 years.
      TIME
      The _____ was more than 2 years ago.

The gap can be filled by the words 'last time I saw him', so you write:

Example: | 0 | L A S T | T I M E | I | S A W | H I M |

Write **only** the missing words **IN CAPITAL LETTERS on the separate answer sheet**.

25   'I'm really sorry I lost your scarf, I promise I'll buy you a new one,' she said to me.
      LOSING
      She _____ and promised to buy a new one.

26   I've reached a decision about what I'm going to do next year.
      UP
      I've _____ about what I'm going to do next year.

27   We need to have the house decorated before we can sell it.
      DECORATING
      The house _____ before we can sell it.

28   It might get cold later so I'd take a jumper if I were you.
      CASE
      You should _____ it gets cold later.

29   You failed the exam because you didn't pay attention in class.
      PAID
      You wouldn't have failed the exam _____ attention in class.

30   Unfortunately, Mike turned down our offer of a job.
      NOT
      Unfortunately, Mike _____ our offer of a job.

Part 5

You are going to read an extract from a guidebook to London in which Debbie Dodie writes about a well-known shopping destination. For questions **31-36**, choose the answer (**A**, **B**, **C** or **D**) which you think fits best according to the text.

Mark your answers **on the separate answer sheet**.

There's no age limit for working out!

Exercise is good for us. This statement is widely accepted and believed by just about everyone. We know that regular exercise improves muscle tone and function and increases our level of fitness; it improves
5 our physical well-being. I've known that for a long time but never quite managed to find the time in my busy life to do regular exercise. I have never been overweight or felt particularly unhealthy so I didn't feel a great need to exercise. What changed my mind at the age of 75 and
10 made me start exercising was reading an article which said that exercise can combat the effects of ageing and improve memory.

Exercise increases oxygen-rich blood flow to the brain and according to the article I read the benefits of this
15 increased blood flow are especially evident for the middle aged and elderly. It's well-known that, in general, exercise improves the heart's ability to pump blood more effectively and increase the amount of oxygen it can carry. The theory is that the elderly and particularly
20 those with coronary artery disease and hypertension often notice loss of memory and a general decline in mental ability because of a reduction in blood flow to the brain. It seems likely that while exercise improves muscle tone and function it has a similar effect on the
25 brain increasing blood flow. One of the benefits of an increased blood flow to areas at the front of the brain is improved memory. And the really good news is that apparently the positive effects of exercise on the brain are immediate and long-lasting.

30 The points discussed in the article had a real effect on me. At my age news like that shouldn't be taken lightly. I thought, well, I've got nothing to lose, so I got myself along to the local gym and asked what they would advise an old man like me to do to keep fit.
35 They were extremely encouraging and helpful, I had been worried they might laugh in my face and send me to the old people's home for yoga classes but not at all. They took me very seriously and gave me a proper assessment, then together we came up with an
40 exercise regime for me. I didn't want to overdo it and I had read that just half an hour of exercise three times a week is sufficient to cause a significant increase in brain power. With that in mind we decided I should start with some gentle exercise on the exercise bike
45 followed by some brisk walking and light jogging on the running machine; a total of 40 minutes exercise 3 times a week. I don't use the weights but now I'm getting more used to it, I'm starting to do ten minutes or so on some of the other machines like the cross-
50 trainer, the stepper and the rowing machine and I really enjoy it.

I don't just confine my exercise to the gym. About once a week I go swimming, which is something I've always enjoyed and done irregularly throughout my life. And
55 if it's a nice day I go for a good brisk walk in the park. I've never been much interested in team sports and it's unrealistic to think that at my age I might suddenly start playing football or tennis or something and I hate the idea of golf, so for me the gym and plain simple
60 exercise is perfect. And does it work? Well, yes I think it does. Since I retired I had started to feel more and more forgetful but now I definitely suffer from that frustration a lot less. I'm sure doing exercise has had a positive effect on my mental health; I simply feel more alert.

31   Why didn't he do exercise when he was younger?
   A   He planned to do exercise after he retired when he had more time.
   B   He didn't feel like it was necessary for him.
   C   He didn't like the idea of doing sport.
   D   He didn't know about the positive effects of exercise.

32   According to the article he read doing exercise helps combat the aging process because
   A   it means that you breathe in more oxygen.
   B   it makes muscles stronger and function better.
   C   it means that less blood and oxygen reach the brain.
   D   it means that more blood and oxygen reach the brain.

33   How did he feel when he went to the gym for the first time?
   A   enthusiastic
   B   nervous
   C   impatient
   D   amused

34   What did the people at the gym do when he asked them for advice?
   A   They helped him plan what sort of exercise he should do and for how long.
   B   They told him to start with yoga classes.
   C   They warned him not to exercise too much.
   D   They suggested doing a little exercise every day.

35   Why does he say 'so for me the gym and plain simple exercise is perfect' in line 59?
   A   Because he doesn't like exercising outside.
   B   Because he's too old to do other sorts of sport he likes.
   C   Because he prefers to exercise by himself.
   D   Because he was never good at other sports.

36   How does he feel since he's started doing exercise?
   A   frustrated
   B   tired
   C   more intelligent
   D   less forgetful

Part 6

You are going to read an article about what makes a good manager. Six sentences have been removed from the article. Choose from the sentences **A-G** the one which fits each gap (**37-42**). There is one extra sentence which you do not need to use.

Mark your answers **on the separate answer sheet**.

Experience, Knowledge, Skills

Being a good manager of people requires excellent communication and interpersonal skills. All people are different and in a working environment there will always be a great mix of personalities and skills. [37]   Like everything in life though, experience brings knowledge and in my many years as both an employee and a manager in various charity organisations I have come to recognise the qualities and skills which make an efficient manager.

I've worked with lots of different people in the past and I think I have experienced all sorts of different types of managers. There are those who are very controlling and always telling you what to do while at the other extreme there are those who are nowhere to be seen. [38]   I think it's important to let people work on their own and not interfere too much; ideally you want to promote assertiveness and self-confidence in your workers and if you are always watching over them and checking up on them they will not develop these skills. At the same time it is not helpful to leave your workers completely alone. The manager is there to oversee things and make sure everything runs smoothly, if employees have a problem or need help they should always be able to ask for it, and the manager should be able to provide it. A line manager who is not available to staff when they need them is of no use at all.

To be an effective manager I think it is important to be optimistic and able to instil a positive attitude in the workforce; the worst kind of manager is one who allows or even encourages a bad feeling in the workplace. [39]   As a result we all lacked confidence in the whole organisation and the office became a very negative environment to work in. It's a manager's responsibility to keep workers' spirits high and create a pleasant atmosphere. Having a naturally optimistic and friendly personality helps.

The best types of managers are those who can accept the responsibility they have been given. If something goes wrong a good manager will take the blame; they are responsible for the team and if the team, or any individual within it, is not performing well then it is ultimately the manager's fault. [40]   They must also then do all they can to solve any unsatisfactory situations and deal with dissatisfaction from higher up in the organisation on the team's behalf.

One thing which managers often do not do enough is give praise. Praise is a very effective management tool and should be exploited as much as possible. [41]   Managers who give a lot of praise are also in a much better situation to criticise when work is not of a satisfactory standard. It is important that employees receive positive as well as negative feedback on their performance; the more feedback there is the more aware workers will be of what is expected of them and positive feedback helps increase motivation. Connected to this last point is the ability to judge on merit. Managers must be able to separate their personal feelings for individuals from their assessment of their work. It is really important to see team members' actions objectively. Any feelings of favouritism or discrimination can be very harmful to the team.

Managers need to be able to recognise the strengths and weaknesses of their employees and use them appropriately. This includes recognising their own strengths and weaknesses. [42]   Managers need to be flexible in their approach to assigning work so that tasks are assigned to those best suited to doing them. I have worked for an organisation where work was given to individuals based on the time of the day they were available to work rather than their personal expertise; this not only resulted in the jobs not being done well, and therefore reduced efficiency, but also great dissatisfaction among workers and clients. For example, someone with excellent computer skills but poor public speaking skills should not be asked to go into schools and universities to give presentations. At the same time it is essential to share knowledge and experience so that the team as a whole develop existing skills and individuals learn new ones.

Finally, empathy is an enormously important quality when working as a manager of people. The basic rule of 'treat others as you would expect others to treat you' is fundamental. It's important to try to put yourself in your colleagues' situation and try and appreciate how they are feeling and then act accordingly.

A They should never promise anything that is not possible as this will lead to disappointment and undermine confidence in the company.

B Now that I work as a manager myself I try to be neither too controlling nor too distant.

C Efficiently managing a team of people is no easy task and there will be many challenging moments.

D In the past I have worked in an office where my line manager was constantly complaining about and criticising the directors of the company.

E Managers should look for examples of good work and congratulate workers accordingly.

F Managers choose and develop their team and so must accept responsibility for the bad as well as the good results of their efforts.

G An efficient team makes the most of all the skills different individuals bring to it.

Part 7

You are going to read an article in which four people talk about their work as teachers. For questions **43-52** choose from the people (**A-D**). The people may be chosen more than once. When more than one answer is required they may be given in any order.

Mark your answers **on the separate answer sheet**.

Which person or people:

has been a teacher the longest?		43
no longer works as a teacher?		44
has taught in many different countries?		45
mentions the qualities which are important to be a good teacher?		46
says they became a teacher because they were not happy in their previous job?		47
says they like working as a teacher because their job is always interesting?	48	49
mentions a difficulty of their subject?		50
says they have had a number of different jobs?		51
says that they had been interested in teaching from a young age?		52

Following One's Vocation

A   Anna

I first got into teaching 4 years ago when I decided to quit my office job and do a bit of travelling. I'd heard of the CELTA qualification to teach English to adults and thought it would be a great way to see the world. I'd also been interested in teaching since I was at school and with the CELTA thought it would be a perfect combination — teaching and travel. Since completing the course I've spent time teaching in the UK, Austria, Poland and Spain and have loved every minute. I've taught people of all ages and levels. I'd say the main thing I enjoy about teaching is the fact that you're able to engage with people from different countries, all of whom have different backgrounds and experiences, and I feel that this therefore makes teaching an interesting, varied profession. I think the thing I found the most frustrating was probably going into different schools and trying to teach children and teenagers who were not interested in learning English and only there because their parents had made them. However, this meant there was always a challenge in trying to find material that these students would be interested in and a job where you don't have challenges I imagine would be rather boring. I've recently started working as a primary school teacher, which I'm really enjoying. I look back on my time teaching abroad with a lot of fondness and for this reason it is something I would definitely like to do again in the future.

B   Valerie

I love teaching because it is never boring. I have been a teacher for over twenty years and I still enjoy my day–to–day work. I teach Science to students aged eleven to sixteen. This sometimes involves explaining difficult concepts and examining ethical questions which some students find very difficult. It is very stimulating working with young people and their enthusiasm and optimism can be quite infectious. To be a good teacher you need to be very knowledgeable about your subject. You must have a good sense of humour and be fair and consistent in your dealings with other people, but most of all you must be a good communicator. There are lots of teachers who know their subject very well but unless you can enthuse your students and build their confidence and self-esteem you will never be an inspirational teacher.

C   Sally

I have been teaching for 3 years now and decided to train to be a food technology teacher after working in the food industry for 5 years. I was fed up with working long hours, knowing the end result was making profit for the company I was working for at the time rather than giving me satisfaction. I have also always loved my subject — Home Economics, Food technology and Cookery — and wanted the opportunity to use my experience and knowledge to inspire and help others. Friends had put me off going into teaching previously due to the notorious heavy workload. It has been the most rewarding and challenging job of my career and I now couldn't imagine doing anything else. I am lucky with my subject because progress and success are instant in practical cookery lessons; giving plenty of opportunity to praise pupils and raise their confidence.
There have been very difficult times in my teaching career, especially the first year, when learning the work-life balance was impossible to grasp; this in conjunction with challenging behavioural issues was a steep learning curve, but I am pleased I persevered. Over time teaching got easier and I think it is the most fulfilling, satisfying profession I could do. The odd pupil that walks out of the class and says 'thanks for a great lesson, Miss' or the look on a pupil's face when his bread comes out of the oven, makes the hard work worth while.

D   Joanna

After studying languages at university, I was unsure what I wanted to do for a living. I worked for a year in a nursery school and, in my spare time, volunteered for a charity that sends people on projects in developing countries. I put together a programme of induction for the volunteers, to prepare them for going on their projects. I soon decided that I would like to do this as a full-time job, but I needed to get a qualification in education and some more experience. I took a postgraduate teacher training course and worked for three years teaching languages in a secondary school. During that time, I got very involved in global education — teaching schoolchildren about global issues and how they affect people in developing countries. After three years of teaching, I got a job managing a global education centre. I co-ordinated and contributed to a programme of workshops for children and training for teachers. A further three years later, the charity I had volunteered for could afford to give me a full-time job, and I've been working there for two years now.

Part 1

You **must** answer this question. Write your answer in **140-190** words in an appropriate style.

1   In your English class you have been talking about technology. Now your English teacher has asked you to write an essay for homework.

Write your essay using **all** the notes and giving reasons for your point of view.

Some people think that in a not-so-far future technology will replace humans in many activities, even in teaching. Do students think this will really happen? What could the pros and cons be for them?

Notes
Write about:
1 working at own speed
2 having no help
3 —————— (your own idea)

Part 2

Write an answer to **one** of the questions **2-5** in this part. Write your answer in **140-190** words in an appropriate style.

2   Your teacher has asked you to write a story for an international magazine. The story must **begin** with the following words:

As soon as I closed the door behind me, all the lights came on.

Write your **story**.

3   You have seen this announcement on an international student website:

My favourite free-time activity

What do you like to do when you're not studying? What is your favourite hobby, why do you enjoy it so much and what does it involve? How did you begin and how much time do you spend doing it?
We'll publish the best articles on the website next month.

Write your **article**.

4   An international film magazine you read is looking for reviews with the following title: 'The last film I watched'. You have decided to write a **review** for the magazine. Describe the film and say what you think about it. Would you recommend it to other people?

Write your **review**.

5   Answer the following question based on the set book you have read.

Sometimes we are not satisfied with the way a book ends. Describe the ending of the book and say whether you were pleased that it ended that way, or whether you would have preferred a different ending.

Write your **essay**.

Part 1

(5) You'll hear people talking in eight different situations. For questions **1-8**, choose the best answer (**A**, **B** or **C**).

1   You hear someone talking about something he saw on television. What did he see?
  A   a magic trick
  B   a drama
  C   a sporting event

2   You hear a woman complaining about something. What is she complaining about?
  A   types of mobile phones
  B   teenagers
  C   the public transport system

3   You hear somebody talking on the phone. What is the purpose of their phone call?
  A   to complain
  B   to arrange to meet someone
  C   to apologise

4   You hear somebody talking in a shop. What kind of shop is it?
  A   a health food shop
  B   a greengrocer's
  C   a chemist's

5   You hear a man talking about his sister. What is his sister's biggest fault?
  A   She talks too much.
  B   She's too serious.
  C   She gets easily annoyed.

6   You hear 2 people talking. What is their relationship?
  A   They're related.
  B   They go to college together.
  C   They go to the same gym.

7   You hear a man talking to his partner on the phone. When is he going to leave work?
  A   8.30
  B   8
  C   9.30

8   What is the speaker describing?
  A   a documentary
  B   a visit to a national park
  C   a friend's holiday

Part 2

(6) You'll hear an information announcement about facilities offered at Blackpool Airport. For questions **9-18**, complete the sentences with a word or short phrase.

Blackpool Airport

The majority of check-in desks at Blackpool Airport are located on [9 _____] of the terminal building.

UK, London and German flights operate from check-in Area 14, which is located on a level beneath [10 _____]

Ensure that carry-on luggage does not contain any liquids, gels or pastes that [11 _____]

Airline staff are on hand if you [12 _____]

Enjoy the comfort and relaxing atmosphere of the Eric Morecambe Lounge for up to three hours for only [13 _____]

A left luggage facility is available in the [14 _____]

Those collecting keys from the car key holding facility must have [15 _____] when collecting the keys.

[16 _____] is served from 4 am.

The airport is conveniently located approximately [17 _____] of Blackpool city centre.

[18 _____] passengers travelled through Blackpool Airport last year.

Part 3

(7) You will hear five different actors talking about their first stage performance. For questions **19-23** choose from the list (**A-H**) to say what each person felt during the performance. Use the letters only once. There are three extra letters which you do not need to use.

A	nervous	Speaker 1	19	
B	proud	Speaker 2	20	
C	excited	Speaker 3	21	
D	calm	Speaker 4	22	
E	exhausted	Speaker 5	23	
F	sick			
G	anxious			
H	astonished			

Part 4

(8)   You will hear an interview with the creator of a web-based music service. For questions **24-30**, choose the best answer (**A**, **B** or **C**).

24   Why is MusicFlow popular with record companies?
    A   It gives users instant access.
    B   It is completely legal.
    C   It has a very big catalogue of music.

25   What is one of Steven Pride's faults?
    A   working too hard
    B   being a pirate
    C   going to sleep at inappropriate times

26   Why does he admire the Beatles?
    A   Because of how many good songs they recorded.
    B   Because they inspired Oasis.
    C   Because of their business acumen.

27   Whose is the latest album you can listen to on MusicFlow?
    A   Little Feat's
    B   The Black Keys'
    C   Leonard Cohen's

28   Where does Steven Pride think most people hear about new music?
    A   from websites
    B   from friends
    C   from the radio

29   What was the first challenge he faced?
    A   making deals with record companies
    B   adding all the new songs
    C   fighting music piracy

30   Who does he believe MusicFlow's main competitors are?
    A   Geezer
    B   Phapster
    C   nobody

Part 1
2 minutes (3 minutes for groups of three)

Good morning/afternoon/evening. My name is _____ and this is my colleague _____.

And your names are?

Can I have your mark sheets, please?

Thank you.

First of all we'd like to know something about you.

- Where are you from, (*Candidate A*)?
- And you, (*Candidate B*)?
- What do you like about living (here / name of candidate's home town)?
- And what about you, (*Candidate A/B*)?

Choose questions from the sections below; ask different questions to each candidate, in any order.

Food and health

- Do you think your diet is healthy? Why? / Why not?
- How often do you eat out? What kind of places do you go to?
- Are you interested in cooking? How often do you cook for your family?
- Are you good at sports? How often do you exercise?
- Do you think there are enough sports facilities in your area?

Friendship

- Do you spend much time with your friends? What do you do together?
- What are the qualities a good friend should have?
- Is it important for friends to be the same age? Why? / Why not?
- Do you think friendship can last forever?
- Is it important for friends to share the same interests? Why? / Why not?

Environment

- Do you think it is important to protect the environment?
- What actions to you usually take to give your contribution?
- Does your school have a programme aimed at protecting the environment?
- Do you live in a city / village that follows 'green' rules? Which are they?
- Would you like to work for the protection of the environment in the future? What would you like to do?

1 Travelling to school **2 Enjoying time with animals**	**Part 2** 4 minutes (6 minutes for groups of three)

Interlocutor   In this part of the test, I'm going to give each of you two photographs.
I'd like you to talk about your photographs on your own for about a minute, and also to answer a question about your partner's photographs.

(*Candidate A*), it's your turn first. Here are your photographs. They show **people travelling to school**.

*Place **Photo 1** in front of Candidate A.*

I'd like you to compare the photographs, and say **what the advantages and disadvantages are of these different ways of travelling to school**.

All right?

Candidate A
🕐 *1 minute*   _____

Interlocutor   Thank you.

(*Candidate B*), **have you ever spent time at the beach?**

Candidate B
🕐 *approximately*   _____
30 seconds

Interlocutor   Thank you.

Now, (*Candidate B*), here are your photographs; they show **they show people and animals**.

*Place **Photo 2** in front of Candidate B.*

I'd like you to compare the photographs, and say **why you think the people are enjoying spending time with these animals**.

All right?

Candidate B
🕐 *1 minute*   _____

Interlocutor   Thank you.

(*Candidate A*), **which one of these animals would you like to keep as a pet?**

Candidate A
🕐 *approximately*   _____
30 seconds

Interlocutor   Thank you.

1 (*Candidate A*)

What are the advantages and disadvantages of these different ways of travelling to school?

1

2 (*Candidate B*)

Why do you think the people are enjoying spending time with these animals?

2

21 Helping the environment and wildlife	**Part 3** 4 minutes (5 minutes for groups of three) **Part 4** 4 minutes (6 minutes for groups of three)

Part 3

Interlocutor

Now, I'd like you to talk about something together for about two minutes (*3 minutes for groups of three*).

Imagine your school's environmental group has decided to do something to help the environment and local wildlife. Here are some of the suggestions for what the group can do and a question for you to discuss. First you have some time to look at the task.

(*The Interlocutor will show the candidates the page with* **Task 21** *and will allow 15 seconds.*)

Now, talk to each other about **how these activities might help the environment and local wildlife.**

Candidates
🕐 *2 minutes*
(3 minutes for groups of three)

Interlocutor

Thank you. Now you have about a minute to decide **which two would be the most effective**.

Candidates
🕐 *1 minute*
(for pairs and groups of three)

Interlocutor

Thank you.

Part 4

Interlocutor

Use the following questions, in order, as appropriate:

- How important is it to protect the environment? Why?
- Do you learn about environmental issues at school?
- Do people in your country regularly recycle waste?
- Do you think we do enough to protect the environment?
- What wildlife species are endangered in your country?
- What is your country and/or your local community doing to help them?

Thank you. That is the end of the test.

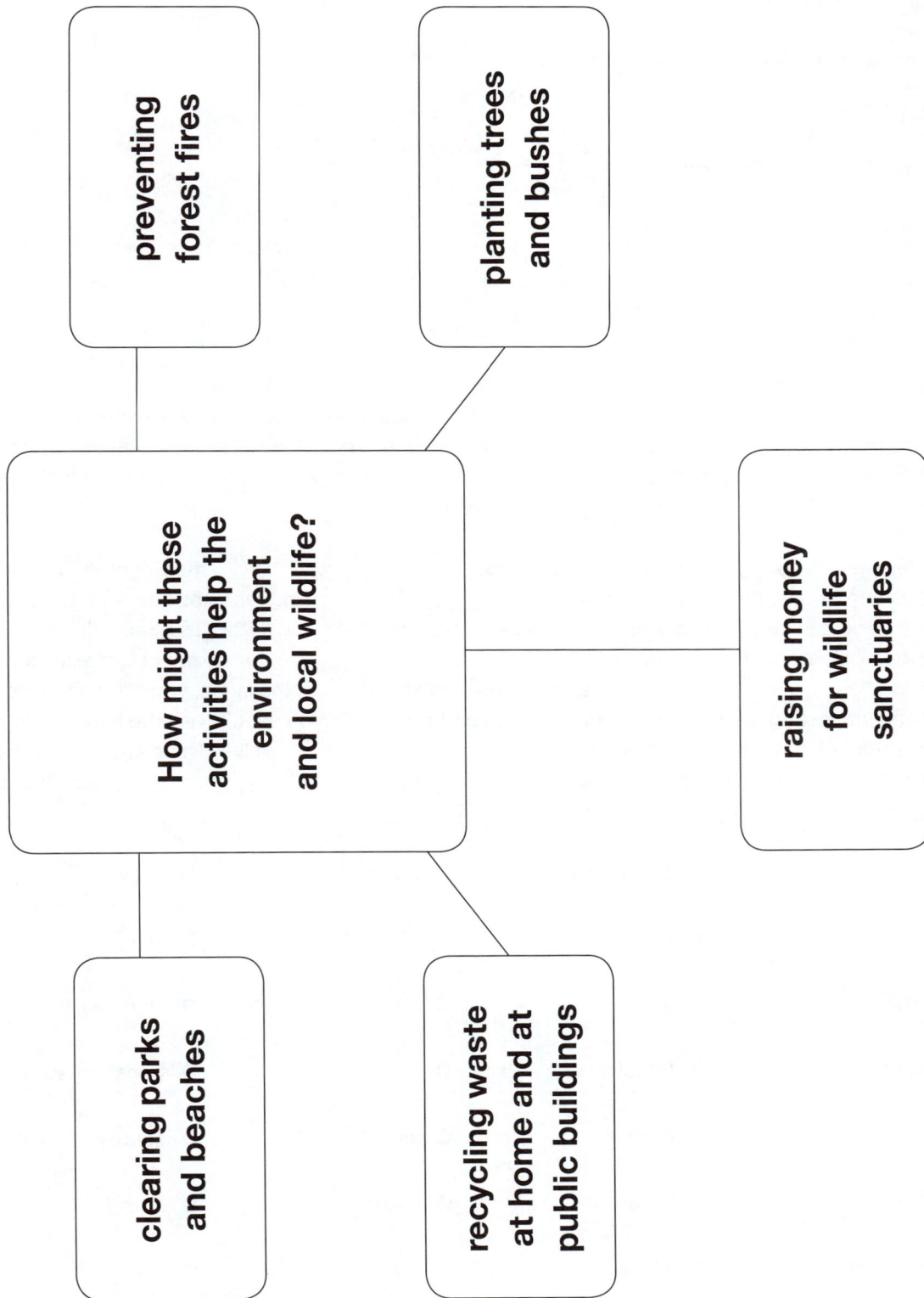

Task 21

preventing forest fires

planting trees and bushes

How might these activities help the environment and local wildlife?

raising money for wildlife sanctuaries

clearing parks and beaches

recycling waste at home and at public buildings

Part 1

For questions **1-8**, read the text below and decide which answer (**A, B, C** or **D**) best fits each gap. There is an example at the beginning (**0**).

Mark your answers **on the separate answer sheet.**

Example:

0   **A** resort   **B** complex   **C** site   **D** place

0	A	B	C	D
	▬	▭	▭	▭

Brighton

This popular seaside (**0**) _____ on the south coast of England is so (**1**) _____ to London it has sometimes been called 'London by the sea'. It is one of the United Kingdom's top ten beach destinations and was recently voted the UK's Green Capital. Brighton has also always had a reputation (**2**) _____ being very stylish and fashionable and in particular 'funky'. It's a very cool place and has plenty to offer every kind of visitor.

Those interested in history or architecture should (**3**) _____ the Brighton Pavilion. Originally a farmhouse, the Pavilion was (**4**) _____ into an exotic seaside home for the Prince Regent, who later became King George IV, between 1815 and 1822. It's a beautiful mixture of Indian and classical architecture and is quite (**5**) _____ in style. For fantastic shopping you should (**6**) _____ an afternoon walking through the lanes; you'll find all sorts of unusual and interesting shops there. If you want fun and good food you should visit the famous Victorian pier. This stretches out over the sea and is (**7**) _____ of life. There are amusement arcades, cafés and shops as well as places to try some very (**8**) _____ fish and chips.

---

1   **A** next   **B** close   **C** convenient   **D** easy

2   **A** to   **B** for   **C** of   **D** with

3   **A** visit   **B** go   **C** look   **D** sightsee

4   **A** translated   **B** transferred   **C** altered   **D** transformed

5   **A** unique   **B** alone   **C** single   **D** solo

6   **A** pass   **B** have   **C** waste   **D** spend

7   **A** complete   **B** whole   **C** full   **D** plenty

8   **A** real   **B** authentic   **C** true   **D** genuine

Part 2

For questions **9-16**, read the text below and think of the word that best fits each gap. Use only one word in each gap. There is an example at the beginning (**0**).

Write your answers **IN CAPITAL LETTERS on the separate answer sheet**.

Example: | 0 | | O | F | | | | | | | | | | | | | | | | | |

World Music Day

The idea (**0**) _____ World Music Day or Fête de la Musique began in France (**9**) _____ the 1980s but has quickly spread across the globe and is now celebrated (**10**) _____ 21st June in over 120 countries.

An American musician, Joel Cohen, who was working for a French radio station, first came up (**11**) _____ the idea for a music festival that everyone could enjoy and take (**12**) _____ in. He suggested an all-night music festival (**13**) _____ celebrate the summer solstice (the longest day). The French minister for culture liked the idea and it first became reality in June 1982. The main idea behind the festival is that music is (**14**) _____ great way to bring people together regardless of their nationality, ethnic and cultural background or age.

It (**15**) _____ extremely popular, particularly because all the events were free.

Today the event is celebrated in cities as far apart as Potsdam and Osaka, New York and Sydney. The day does not only involve individual musicians but also orchestras, cultural organisations, and schools. The best thing (**16**) _____ the festival is that musicians are encouraged to perform outside the usual music venues and concert halls. Whole towns are turned into huge outdoor concerts. And every kind of music is on offer. You can hear classical music, jazz bands, rock groups, pop bands, folk music and singer-songwriters all in the same place, and all for free.

Part 3

For questions **17-24** read the text below. Use the word given in capitals at the end of some of the lines to form a word that fits in the gap **in the same line**. There is an example at the beginning (**0**).

Write your answers **IN CAPITAL LETTERS on the separate answer sheet.**

Example: | 0 | S | T | R | A | N | G | E | R | S | | | | | | | | | |

Flat sharing

Sharing your living space is never easy but is it better to share with family or
friends or complete (**0**) _____? Living with your family is   STRANGE
certainly not (**17**) _____; it can cause all sorts of problems,   COMPLICATE
but at least with your family you know the other people in your house very well.
And generally you like each other and try to be nice to each other. At some point
though most of us want some (**18**) _____ and so we end up   DEPEND
moving out of the family home.

Nowadays it is unusual for young people to be able to afford to rent somewhere
by themselves and living alone can be frightening and lonely,
(**19**) _____ if it is in a strange new city, so lots of people   SPECIAL
decide to share. If you have friends in the same place in similar situations then it
makes sense to live together and this can be very (**20**) _____.   SUCCESS
However, living with someone will put all kinds of pressures on your
(**21**) _____.   FRIEND

You find out all sorts of things about someone when you share the same living
room, kitchen and bathroom. Choice of TV programme,
(**22**) _____ and length of time spent in the bathroom are   TIDY
all common causes of (**23**) _____. Sometimes it is better   AGREE
to move in with someone who is not your friend. That way their annoying (**24**)
_____ will not change an existing relationship and if you get   BEHAVE
on they could become a new friend.

Part 4

For questions **25-30**, complete the second sentence so that it has a similar meaning to the first sentence, using the word given. **Do not change the word given**. You must use between **two** and **five** words, including the word given. Here is an example (**0**).

Example:

0   I haven't seen him for at least 2 years.

     TIME

     The _____ was more than 2 years ago.

The gap can be filled by the words 'last time I saw him', so you write:

Example: | 0 | | L | A | S | T | | T | I | M | E | | I | | S | A | W | | H | I | M |

Write **only** the missing words **IN CAPITAL LETTERS on the separate answer sheet**.

25   As long as there isn't a problem with traffic we'll be there in half an hour.

     IF

     We'll be there in half an hour _____ any problems with traffic.

26   A professional is going to do her make-up for her.

     HAVE

     She's going to _____ by a professional.

27   It was a very bad idea to spend so much money on a new TV.

     SHOULD

     You _____ so much money on a new TV.

28   'It's icy so please be careful when you go out,' Joe's mother said.

     WARNED

     Joe's mother _____ careful when he went out because it was icy.

29   I think you should ask your teacher for help.

     WOULD

     If I _____ ask your teacher for help.

30   Mark left the flat before Lauren got home.

     ALREADY

     When Lauren got home Mark _____ the flat.

Part 5

You are going to read an article about the green and innovative city of Curitiba in Brazil. For questions **31-36** choose the answer (**A**, **B**, **C** or **D**) which you think fits best according to the text.

Mark your answers **on the separate answer sheet**.

A Sustainable City

One city which has always had the environment as its top priority is the Brazilian city of Curitiba. It is in the south of the country and is one of the most innovative cities in the world. It is so environmentally-
5 friendly it is known as the ecological capital of Brazil. The people in Curitiba are very proud of their city and not only believe in a greener lifestyle but they really live it. Sustainable development is evident in all aspects of city life.

10 Residents have planted 1.6 million trees and over 70% of all waste is recycled. Curitiba has the highest rate of paper and glass recycling of anywhere in Brazil. Paper recycling in Curitiba saves over 1,000 trees a year. Like many cities in the world Curitiba
15 also faces many socio-economic problems but because it is such a unique and forward-thinking city the residents came up with a revolutionary idea to help poor families and reduce waste at the same time. Each family sorts its rubbish and then
20 it is weighed and 'sold' back to the city council in exchange for fruit and meat. This provides healthy food for those who can't afford it and also encourages recycling and helps keep the city clean and tidy. Rubbish which cannot be recycled is burnt
25 to make electricity.

The city's public transport is also one of the greenest in the world. The bus service is cheap and efficient and saves millions of car journeys each year as you can use the buses to get anywhere in the city. There

are over 70 kilometres of bus-only routes through   30
the city. Roads have 4 lanes, 2 for cars and lorries and 2 for buses only. This means buses can run freely through the city without getting stuck in traffic jams. As a result millions of people use the bus every day rather than their cars. The best thing, though,   35
is that the 1,200 buses which make up the network run on biodiesel; that is fuel made from plants like soya. Reduced car traffic and low consumption of traditional fuels means that Curitiba is one of the least polluted cities in Brazil.   40

Curitiba has grown dramatically over the years. In 1950 300,000 people lived there, now the population is 1.8 million. The architect who led the city's growth in the 1960s was so popular he later became the city's mayor. One big challenge that the city has   45
faced throughout its development is flooding. The city has had to find ways to protect itself from flooding which has affected the city centre for many years. Curitiba wanted to find a solution which worked with nature. The solution they came up with   50
involved creating a number of lakes in the city's parks which could hold flood water. Also no buildings were allowed to be built in areas which had a risk of flooding. One of the most beautiful buildings in the city is the university. It is called the Free University of   55
Environment and was built using recycled eucalyptus poles. You can study a wide range of subjects there although of course it offers many different environmental courses, including bio-architecture.

31   Why is Curitiba known as the ecological capital of Brazil?

   A   It is a very modern and new city.

   B   It has a lot of green spaces.

   C   The people there do a lot to protect and conserve the environment.

   D   It is visited by lots of foreigners interested in the environment.

32   What does the author mean in line 17 when it says the residents 'came up with a revolutionary idea'?

   A   Their idea made a lot of people angry.

   B   Their idea was original and different.

   C   Their idea caused a lot of political change.

   D   Their idea made a lot of money for the city.

33   Which of the following does not happen in Curitiba?

   A   Families separate their household waste.

   B   Residents are given food as a reward for recycling their rubbish.

   C   Residents help to keep the city clean and tidy.

   D   Recycled waste is used to produce electricity.

34   Why don't many people in Curitiba use cars?

   A   Because the public transport system is so efficient.

   B   Because there are too many traffic jams.

   C   Because many roads in the city are for buses only.

   D   Because fuel is very expensive.

35   Why does Curitiba have less pollution than other cities?

   A   It is smaller than other cities.

   B   Cars use fuel which doesn't cause pollution.

   C   People don't use cars much and buses use fuel which doesn't cause much pollution.

   D   There are only 1,200 buses in the city.

36   How did the city solve the problem of flooding?

   A   by building fewer buildings

   B   by making sure there were lots of lakes

   C   by creating more parks

   D   They didn't do anything but hoped nature would solve the problem itself.

Part 6

You are going to read an article about our relationship with time. Six sentences have been removed from the article. Choose from the sentences **A-G** the one which fits each gap (**37-42**). There is one extra sentence which you do not need to use.

Mark your answers **on the separate answer sheet**.

Time for a Change

How many times do you hear people say they don't have time to do something? All the time! 'I meant to do that but I didn't have time!' is something we say or think far too often; it is the number one excuse for not doing something we should have done. **37** This is a relationship which has also changed a lot through history. Think about all the machines and time-saving gadgets that are now a part of our everyday life that people living 100 or even 50 years ago had to do without; computers, washing machines, vacuum cleaners, microwaves and dishwashers are just a few. We have mobile phones now so that we can contact each other at any time no matter where we are, the Internet gives us access to just about any information we could possibly want as well as providing instant communication with other people anywhere in the world. **38**

The idea of using time efficiently has become increasingly important in the Western world. People in wealthy developed countries are often expected to do several jobs at once. At a time when unemployment is high and international competition is strong there is a lot of pressure on companies and individual workers to be as efficient as possible and to get as much work done as possible in the limited time available. **39** This concept of time pressure has also been passed on to the less developed countries where many of the goods for developing countries are made. In places like India and Mexico people often have to work very long shifts, sometimes as much as 12 to 16 hours a day, or even for 48 hours without a break. Goods have to be produced to meet demand in the developed world and this demand puts a lot of pressure on workers. Time is increasingly becoming a commodity like any other. **40** Do you use the self-service checkout in the supermarket? Have you bought furniture and then assembled it yourself at home? Have you spent time setting up a new computer?

If you have then you have been working for free. It is possible to buy and sell time these days. For example, you can pay someone else to do your shopping for you or walk your dog for you if you don't have time, but it won't be cheap. A positive reflection of how our relationship with time is changing is that in some cities there are things called time banks where you can exchange time with other busy people. **41** You will then be paid back in time when you need it. No money changes hands but everyone has to pay into the bank in time.

The biggest challenge we face in our personal lives is how not to waste time and make the most of the time we have. According to recent research 20% of people regularly cancel social arrangements because of a lack of time and men do this more often than women. However, cancelling social arrangements can have a serious negative impact because it reduces our quality of life; it can stop us doing what we want, which can lead to unhappiness. **42** This doesn't have to be something active or sociable; it might be finding time to read a good book. By making sure we don't miss out on the things we enjoy and value we are likely to be happier and more satisfied with life in general.

A   In spite of these new inventions we still run out of time.

B   If you have some free time you can volunteer to do something for someone else like wait for a delivery or water their plants while they are on holiday.

C   As a result working hours have increased by 25% in the USA and in Japan workers sometimes sleep in the office.

D   Time is money and nowadays many companies try to save time and money by making their customers work for free.

E   Time is a very precious commodity and humans have always had a very close relationship with it.

F   This doesn't mean we should put off things which are boring or difficult just because we don't want to do them.

G   It is important to find time for ourselves to do the things which matter most to us.

Part 7

You are going to read an article in which four people talk about cheating in exams. For questions **43-52** choose from the people (**A-D**). The people may be chosen more than once. When more than one answer is required they may be given in any order.

Mark your answers **on the separate answer sheet**.

Which person or people:

was caught cheating in an exam?	43
didn't let a friend copy their work?	44
regrets trying to cheat in an exam?	45
cheated more than once?	46 47
tried to cheat by writing notes on a part of their body?	48
decided not to cheat again after a bad experience?	49 50
thinks it is always wrong to cheat?	51
thinks there is nothing wrong with cheating?	52

Cheating in exams

A

This happened when I was about 14 years old. The last exam of the year was history, which had always been my worst subject. I was useless at remembering dates and people's names so I decided to write the dates and names of the important events we'd studied on the inside of my arm and then wore a jumper to cover it up so no-one could see. Unfortunately though, it was a really hot day. I really wanted to take my jumper off but I couldn't. I realised after about ten minutes that there was no way I would be able to look at what I'd written without the teacher seeing and I just wished I hadn't done it. I felt so hot and uncomfortable and was really worried about the teacher seeing and catching me that I didn't do very well in the test at all. I was too distracted. I think I probably would have got a better result if I hadn't tried to cheat. I learnt a good lesson though. I never tried to cheat again after that.

B

My friend and I had the same surname so we always ended up sitting next to each other, or one behind the other, in exams at school. We worked out this system where we would pass a piece of paper to each other with the answers to the questions. Sometimes we just passed it by hand if we were sitting close enough and other times we'd throw it on the floor for the other person to pick up. It was quite a good system and I think over lots of exams we probably helped each other equally so it was fair and I'm sure we both got higher marks. Unfortunately a teacher did see us doing it once. I was just leaning down to pick up a paper my friend was passing back to me when a teacher appeared out of nowhere and picked it up first. There was no way we could deny what we were doing, it was so obvious. The teacher didn't say anything until the end of the exam and then when she collected our papers she wrote a big zero at the top. We didn't do it anymore after that, it had been good before but we decided it wasn't worth the risk.

C

I used to always cheat in my maths exams when I was at school. We were allowed to take a calculator with us into the exam and I used to write all the important formulae that we were supposed to remember on the inside of the calculator case. I did it lots of times. I don't regret it at all. I was quite good at maths anyway but I'm sure I got better results as a result of cheating. In other exams like chemistry and physics, I sometimes wrote notes on bits of tissue then pretended I needed to blow my nose and looked at my notes during the exam. It worked really well. There was only one time I was almost caught; I dropped the tissue on the floor by accident just as a teacher was walking past. He was about to pick it up when my friend, who had also seen what had happened, deliberately knocked over his water bottle. The teacher was so busy clearing up the water I think he forgot about me. If you're clever enough to work out a way to cheat and not get caught then I think you deserve to get good marks. It's like that in the real world; if you can do something more easily and with less hard work then you will. Why not?

D

I've never cheated in an exam and really don't see the point. I mean sooner or later people will find out if you know something or not. If you cheat to get better results then you're lying to yourself as well as to everyone else. Rather than spending your time thinking of really clever and original ways to cheat without anyone realising, you should just spend that time studying. I'm sure it will help you a lot more in the long run. A friend once tried to read my answers in an exam while pretending to pick something up off the floor. As soon as I realised I covered my work so he couldn't see. He was quite annoyed with me afterwards but I didn't think it was fair that he should do well because of my hard work.

Part 1

You **must** answer this question. Write your answer in **140-190** words in an appropriate style.

1   In your English class you have been talking about friendship. Now your English teacher has asked you to write an essay for homework.

Write your essay using **all** the notes and giving reasons for your point of view.

Some parents think it is one of their duties to choose their children's friends. Is their attitude good or bad?

Notes
Write about:
1 protecting children
2 having less freedom
3 _____ (your own idea)

Part 2

Write an answer to **one** of the questions **2-5** in this part. Write your answer in **140-190** words in an appropriate style on the opposite page. Put the question number in the box at the top of the page.

2   You recently attended an English language course in the UK. You have just received the following email.

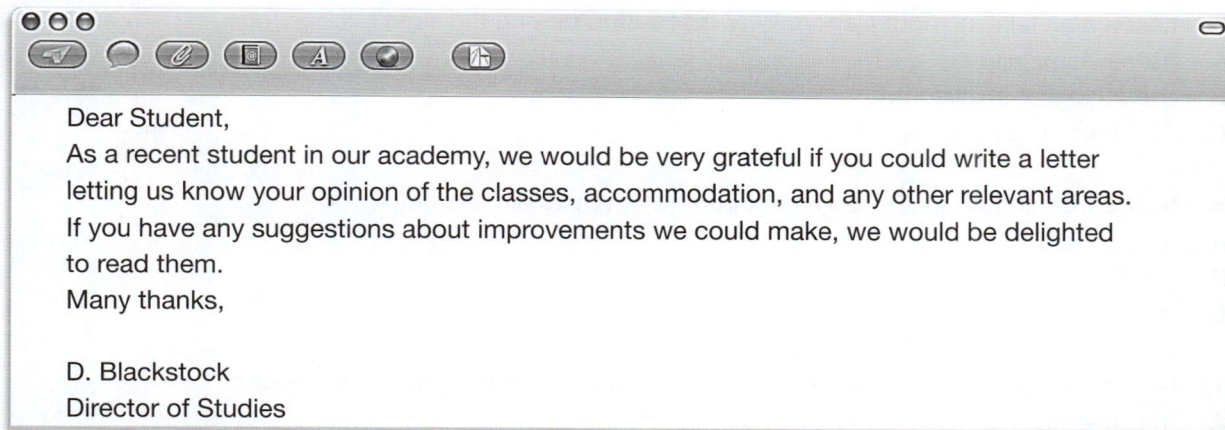

Dear Student,

As a recent student in our academy, we would be very grateful if you could write a letter letting us know your opinion of the classes, accommodation, and any other relevant areas. If you have any suggestions about improvements we could make, we would be delighted to read them.

Many thanks,

D. Blackstock
Director of Studies

Write your **letter**.

3   An English language magazine has invited its readers to write an article about what their lives would be like without computers.

       Write your **article**.

4   Your teacher has asked you to write a **story** for the school magazine. The story must **begin** with the words:

       Ivan had never been so envious of anybody in his life.

       Write your **story**.

5   Answer the following question based on the set book you have read. Write the number 5 in the question box on the opposite page.

       A local bookshop has asked its customers to write a review of a book, to include in its annual catalogue.

       Write your **review**.

Part 1

(9) You'll hear people talking in eight different situations. For questions **1-8**, choose the best answer, (**A**, **B** or **C**).

1   You hear a man talking about a sport. Why did he stop playing the sport?
    A   Because of injury.
    B   He no longer enjoyed it.
    C   He doesn't have enough time.

2   You hear a woman talking about a recent purchase. Where did she buy it?
    A   in a shop
    B   on the Internet
    C   at a local market

3   You hear somebody talking about a new school. What does the person think about it?
    A   It is needed.
    B   It isn't needed.
    C   It's too far away.

4   You hear a woman talking about her job. What is she worried about?
    A   She doesn't have the necessary skills.
    B   She has too much work to do.
    C   She might lose her job.

5   You hear an advertisement for a holiday. What kind of holiday is being advertised?
    A   a cruise
    B   a safari
    C   an activity holiday

6   You hear somebody discussing a radio programme. What kind of programme was it?
    A   a political debate
    B   a quiz programme
    C   a comedy

7   You hear somebody talking about a piece of furniture. How does he feel about it?
    A   It's too big.
    B   It was difficult to assemble.
    C   It was too expensive.

8   You hear somebody talking about their plans for the weekend. What are they going to see?
    A   a concert
    B   a film
    C   a football match

Part 2

(10) You'll hear a talk about an arts festival. For questions **9-18**, complete the sentences with a word or short phrase.

At Art Fair

Brian Daniels is the [9   ] of the Wentworth Art Fair.

The Marta Costello collection is made up of approximately [10   ] drawings, journals, letters, paintings and other items.

Some experts on the artist's work have questioned [11   ] of the collection.

A three-day pass is [12   ]

Doors open at [13   ]

The moderator will be Michael Edward Hall, art historian, critic and correspondent for
[14   ]

Welsh artist Phillipa West is among the most popular and beloved [15   ]
of the 20th century.

The Welsh Arts Council has designated her work 'National Patrimony' and restricted its
[16   ]

The collection became the focus of numerous articles in [17   ] in Europe.

The Wentworth Art Fair Symposium will look into the issues surrounding the collection and its still
[18   ]

Part 3

(11) You will hear five different people talking about a television programme. For questions **19-23**, choose from the list (**A-H**) what each person says about it. Use the letters only once. There are three extra letters which you do not need to use.

A	knows one of the contestants	Speaker 1 19
B	watched it in the past but not now	Speaker 2 20
C	can't understand why people watch it	Speaker 3 21
D	has never watched it	Speaker 4 22
E	watches it regularly	Speaker 5 23
F	watches it occasionally	
G	never felt guilty about watching it	
H	doesn't know anyone who watches it	

Part 4

(12) You will hear an interview with a psychologist about sharing houses. For questions **24-30**, choose the best answer (**A**, **B** or **C**).

24 When do most people share accommodation?
   A When they leave home.
   B When they are invited to.
   C When they are having problems.

25 According to Dr. Millington, what is an important thing to do when sharing a flat?
   A to share food
   B to have established rules
   C to be sociable

26 What is the most common problem with sharing accommodation?
   A paying bills
   B meal times
   C being clean

27 What problem with rotas is mentioned?
   A They are too obvious.
   B You have to pay for them.
   C Circumstances can change.

28 What does she say about having your own space?
   A It's haven.
   B It's tough.
   C It's important.

29 What can be a problem with living with friends?
   A You could have an argument.
   B You trust them too much.
   C It feels strange.

30 What is a fundamental requirement of sharing a flat?
   A being considerate
   B liking the same music
   C enjoying parties

Part 1
2 minutes (3 minutes for groups of three)

Good morning/afternoon/evening. My name is ——————— and this is my colleague ———————.

And your names are?

Can I have your mark sheets, please?

Thank you.

First of all we'd like to know something about you.

- Where are you from, (*Candidate A*)?
- And you, (*Candidate B*)?
- What do you like about living (here / name of candidate's home town)?
- And what about you, (*Candidate A/B*)?

Select one or more questions from any of the following categories, as appropriate.

People you know

- Do you have a best friend? What do you like about him/her?
- How do you stay in touch with your friends?
- How often do you have disagreements with your friends? What normally happens after these disagreements?
- How easy is it to you to make friends?

Things you like

- What's your favourite subject at school? Why do you like it?
- Do you like reading? What do you like to read? Why?
- Do you enjoy listening to music in your free time? Why? / Why not?
- Tell us about the things you like doing at the weekend.

Places you go to

- Do you like your school? Why? / Why not?
- Are there any nice places to go in your area? What are they? Why do you like them?
- Have you been anywhere nice recently? Where did you go? Why?
- Where would you like to go for your next holiday? Who would you like to go with?

1 People enjoying nature 2 People spending time outside	**Part 2** 4 minutes (6 minutes for groups of three)

Interlocutor   In this part of the test, I'm going to give each of you two photographs. I'd like you to talk about your photographs on your own for about a minute, and also to answer a question about your partner's photographs.

(Candidate A), it's your turn first. Here are your photographs. They show **people enjoying nature**.

Place **Photo 1** in front of Candidate A.

I'd like you to compare the photographs, and say **why you think the people have chosen to spend time in these places**.

All right?

Candidate A
🕐 1 minute
_____

Interlocutor   Thank you.

(Candidate B), **do you like looking at wildlife?**

Candidate B
🕐 approximately
   30 seconds
_____

Interlocutor   Thank you.

Now, (Candidate B), here are your photographs. They show **people spending time outside in different situations**.

Place **Photo 2** in front of Candidate B.

I'd like you to compare the photographs, and say **what you think the people are enjoying about spending time outside in these situations**.

All right?

Candidate B
🕐 1 minute
_____

Interlocutor   Thank you.

(Candidate A), **which of these things would you prefer to do? Why?**

Candidate A
🕐 approximately
   30 seconds
_____

Interlocutor   Thank you.

1 (*Candidate A*)

Why do you think people have chosen to spend time in these places?

2 *(Candidate B)*

What are these people enjoying in these situations?

2

21 Summer Jobs	**Part 3** 4 minutes (5 minutes for groups of three)
	Part 4 4 minutes (6 minutes for groups of three)

Part 3

Interlocutor	Now, I'd like you to talk about something together for about two minutes (*3 minutes for groups of three*).
	Imagine you are going to do a summer job. Here are some summer jobs ideas that young people can do in the summer and a question for you to discuss. First you have some time to look at the task.
	(*The Interlocutor will show the candidates the page with **Task 21** and will allow 15 seconds.*)
	Now, talk to each other about **how useful these jobs might be for the people doing them.**
Candidates 🕐 *2 minutes (3 minutes for groups of three)*	
Interlocutor	Thank you. Now you have about a minute to decide **which two are the best choices for summer jobs.**
Candidates 🕐 *1 minute (for pairs and groups of three)*	
Interlocutor	Thank you.

Part 4

Interlocutor	Use the following questions, in order, as appropriate:
	• Do you believe working in the summer is good for young people?
	• What job would you most like to do in the future? Why?
	• Do you think it is a good idea to do the same job as your parents or anyone in your family?
	• Do you think getting a job is difficult nowadays?
	• What do you think the most important factor is when choosing a job?
	• How important is experience in your opinion?
	Thank you. That is the end of the test.

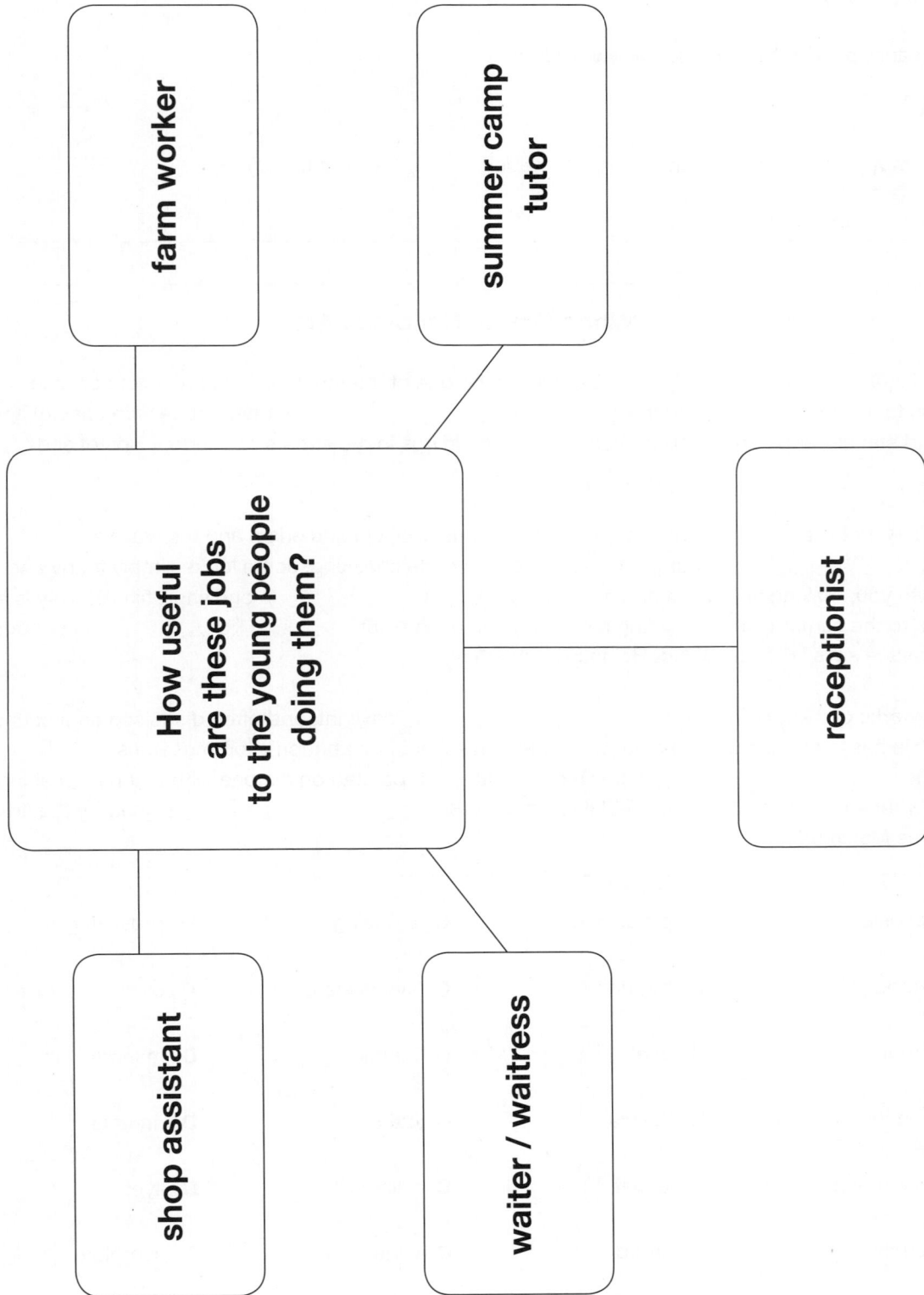

Task 21

farm worker

summer camp tutor

How useful
are these jobs
to the young people
doing them?

receptionist

shop assistant

waiter / waitress

Part 1

For questions **1-8**, read the text below and decide which answer (**A**, **B**, **C** or **D**) best fits each gap. There is an example at the beginning (**0**).

Mark your answers **on the separate answer sheet**.

Example:

| 0 | **A** firstly | **B** greatly | **C** widely | **D** not mostly |

| 0 | A | B | C | D |

When Graffiti Becomes Art

Banksy is (**0**) _____ believed to be one of the most exciting artists of our time. His art is funny, political and thought- (**1**) _____. It is often made with cans of spray paint and stencils and can be found on the side of buildings in the streets of London, Bristol and (**2**) _____ the world.

Banksy's work is about questioning authority, the status quo, consumerism and the way we (**3**) _____ our planet. Some of it is quite shocking, some looks simply funny and then stays with you, making you question your (**4**) _____. In one short film Banksy is seen, his back to the camera, spray painting a message on a blank (**5**) _____ in London. The message says 'The Joy of Not Being Sold Anything.'

Banksy works quickly, often in (**6**) _____ daylight, and often disguised as a council worker. He has even managed to smuggle some of his work into London's top museums. Most (**7**) _____ a piece of 'neolithic art' painted on a stone with a hunter pushing a supermarket shopping trolley. This 'neolithic art' was (**8**) _____ signed by the artist 'Banksyus Maximus'.

| 1 | **A** evoking | **B** producing | **C** arousing | **D** provoking |

| 2 | **A** throughout | **B** through | **C** everywhere | **D** over |

| 3 | **A** treat | **B** deal | **C** handle | **D** manage |

| 4 | **A** reasons | **B** beliefs | **C** ideas | **D** dreams |

| 5 | **A** pamphlet | **B** leaflet | **C** billboard | **D** flyer |

| 6 | **A** bright | **B** broad | **C** wide | **D** complete |

| 7 | **A** lately | **B** early | **C** shortly | **D** recently |

| 8 | **A** even | **B** still | **C** yet | **D** ever |

Part 2

For questions **9-16**, read the text below and think of the word which best fits each gap. Use only **one** word in each gap. There is an example at the beginning (**0**).

Write your answers **IN CAPITAL LETTERS on the separate answer sheet**.

Example: | 0 | | O | N | | | | | | | | | | | | | | | | | |

Into the Dragon's Den

The Dragon's Den is the name of a popular TV show on the BBC which is having an effect
(**0**) _____ the wider business world and encouraging a whole new generation of
entrepreneurs and inventors to follow their dreams.

The show is hosted by five of the UK's top business people, all of (**9**) _____ are very
successful, very rich and very scary. Dragons in human form! In order to get (**10**) _____
the show you have to submit your idea for a new business or your new invention to the BBC.
The thousands of applications are then sorted (**11**) _____ and if you are lucky you will
be chosen to present your idea on the show. Then comes the really terrifying bit.

You have to stand up in front of the Dragons and sell them your idea while you are (**12**) _____
filmed for a national TV show with millions (**13**) _____ viewers. If the Dragons like your
idea then they will invest some of (**14**) _____ own money in your business. Often the
Dragons give the thumbs (**15**) _____, but other times they are prepared to invest
tens (**16**) _____ thousands of pounds.
The Dragon's Den has inspired many people to follow their business dreams.

Part 3

For questions **17-24** read the text below. Use the word given in capitals at the end of some of the lines to form a word that fits in the gap **in the same line**. There is an example at the beginning (**0**).

Write your answers **IN CAPITAL LETTERS on the separate answer sheet**.

Example: | 0 | S | P | I | R | I | T | U | A | L | | | | | | | | | |

The Pilgrimage to Santiago de Compostela

Every year, two hundred thousand pilgrims walk for hundreds of kilometres
to the Sanctuary at Santiago de Compostela. The journey they make is

(**0**) _____, rich in tradition, and passes through   **SPIRIT**
(**17**) _____ landscape.   **PHENOMENON**

The most (**18**) _____ pilgrims' route is the one which starts   **LEGEND**
in France, leaving from Roncevaux (Navarre) and arriving in Santiago.
It is 800 kilometres long and crosses the Pyrenees mountains.
The oldest path is the northern route which follows the

(**19**) _____ coast of Spain with its rias, or drowned river   **SPECTACLE**
valleys, unique to this part of the world. To show the way, the path is
(**20**) _____ with pictures of yellow scallop shells on blue   **MARK**
backgrounds which symbolise the pilgrims.

In the past, pilgrims (**21**) _____ to Santiago followed a   **WALK**
route marked by the Milky Way. These (**22**) _____ pilgrims   **EARLY**
included Saint Frances of Assisi (1182-1226), the Patron saint of Italy. In 1989,
Pope John Paul II went to Santiago to meet a (**23**) _____ of   **CONGREGATE**
over half a million young people who had gathered there from all over the world.
Today, pilgrims who make the journey receive a credencial, a certificate stating
that they are making the pilgrimage. Once they reach Santiago they are

(**24**) _____ the Compostela, a certificate in Latin which   **AWARD**
declares that they have completed the pilgrimage. Just like passing an exam!

Part 4

For questions **25-30**, complete the second sentence so that it has a similar meaning to the first sentence, using the word given. **Do not change the word given.** You must use between **two** and **five** words, including the word given. Here is an example (**0**).

Example:

0   Our neighbour took us into town.
         TAKEN
         We _____ our neighbour.

The gap can be filled by the words 'were taken into town by', so you write:

Example: | 0 | W E R E | T A K E N | I N T O | T O W N | B Y |

Write **only** the missing words **IN CAPITAL LETTERS on the separate answer sheet.**

25   I'll never go to that restaurant again.
         LAST
         That's _____ I will ever go to that restaurant.

26   I'm really looking forward to my holidays.
         WAIT
         I _____ my holidays to come.

27   I regret saying such nasty things.
         WISH
         I _____ such nasty things.

28   It was a mistake to invest in property that year.
         SHOULD
         John _____ in property that year.

29   They are collecting money to build a children's hospital.
         BEING
         Money _____ to build a children's hospital.

30   We repaired the roof to stop it from leaking.
         SO
         We repaired the roof _____ leak.

Part 5

You are going to read an extract from a novel. For questions **31-36**, choose the answer (**A**, **B**, **C** or **D**) which you think fits best according to the text.

Mark your answers **on the separate answer sheet**.

An Extract from *Emma*

One morning, about ten days after Mrs Churchill's decease, Emma was called downstairs to Mr Weston, who could not stay five minutes, and wanted particularly to speak with her. He met her at the parlour-door, and
5 hardly asking her how she did, in the natural key of his voice, sunk it immediately, to say, unheard by her father: 'Can you come to Randalls at any time this morning? Do, if it be possible. Mrs Weston wants to see you. She must see you.'
10 'Is she unwell?'
'No, no, not at all – only a little agitated. She would have ordered the carriage, and come to you, but she must see you alone, and that you know,' nodding towards her father, 'Humph! – Can you come?'
15 'Certainly. This moment, if you please. It is impossible to refuse what you ask in such a way. But what can be the matter? Is she really not ill?'
'Depend upon me – but ask no more questions. You will know it all in time. The most unaccountable business!
20 But hush, hush!'

To guess what all this meant, was impossible even for Emma. Something really important seemed announced by his looks; but, as her friend was well, she endeavoured not to be uneasy, and settling it with her father, that she
25 would take her walk now, she and Mr Weston were soon out of the house together and on their way at a quick pace for Randalls.
'Now,' said Emma, when they were fairly beyond the sweep gates, 'now Mr Weston, do let me know what
30 has happened.'
'No, no,' he gravely replied. 'Don't ask me. I promised my wife to leave it all to her. She will break it to you better than I can. Do not be impatient, Emma; it will all come out too soon.'
35 'Break it to me,' cried Emma, standing still with terror. 'Good God! Mr Weston, tell me at once. Something has happened in Brunswick Square. I know it has. Tell me, I charge you tell me this moment what it is.'
'No, indeed you are mistaken.'
40 'Mr Weston do not trifle with me. Consider how many of my dearest friends are now in Brunswick Square. Which of them is it? I charge you by all that is sacred, not to attempt concealment.'
'Upon my word, Emma.'
45 'Your word! Why not your honour! Why not say upon your honour, that it has nothing to do with any of them?

Good Heavens! What can be to be broke to me, that does not relate to one of that family?'
'Upon my honour,' said he very seriously, 'it does not. It is not in the smallest degree connected with any human 50 being of the name of Knightley.'
Emma's courage returned, and she walked on.

'I was wrong,' he continued, 'in talking of its being broke to you. I should not have used the expression. In fact, it does not concern you – it concerns only myself, 55 that is, we hope. Humph! In short, my dear Emma, there is no occasion to be so uneasy about it. I don't say that it is not a disagreeable business – but things might be much worse. If we walk fast, we shall soon be at Randalls.' 60
Emma found that she must wait; and now it required little effort. She asked no more questions therefore, merely employed her own fancy, and that soon pointed out to her the probability of its being some money concern, something just come to light, of a disagreeable nature 65 in the circumstances of the family, something which the late event at Richmond had brought forward. Her fancy was very active. Half a dozen natural children, perhaps – and poor Frank cut off! This, though very undesirable, would be no matter of agony to her. It inspired little more 70 than an animating curiosity.

'Who is that gentleman on horseback?' said she, as they proceeded speaking more to assist Mr Weston in keeping his secret, than with any other view.
'I do not know. One of the Otways. Not Frank; it is not 75 Frank, I assure you. You will not see him. He is half way to Windsor by this time.'
'Has your son been with you, then?'
'Oh! yes – did not you know? Well, well, never mind.'
For a moment he was silent; and then added, in a tone 80 much more guarded and demure:
'Yes, Frank came over this morning, just to ask us how we did.'
They hurried on, and were speedily at Randalls. 'Well, my dear,' said he, as they entered the room, 'I have brought 85 her, and now I hope you will soon be better. I shall leave you together. There is no use in delay. I shall not be far off, if you want me.' And Emma distinctly heard him add, in a lower tone, before he quitted the room, 'I have been as good as my word. She has not the least idea.' 90
Emma by Jane Austen (1775-1817)

31   When Mr Weston first spoke to Emma
    A   he whispered.
    B   he coughed.
    C   he murmured.
    D   he stuttered.

32   Despite Emma's insistence, Mr Weston refuses to
    A   mind his own business.
    B   accompany Emma in the carriage.
    C   take Emma's father with them.
    D   say what the matter is.

33   When Mr Weston says his wife will break the news to her, Emma is
    A   annoyed.
    B   relieved.
    C   alarmed.
    D   amused.

34   How does Mr Weston manage to calm Emma down?
    A   By taking her back to the house in Brunswick Square.
    B   By explaining that he isn't directly involved.
    C   By giving her his word that no harm has come to anyone.
    D   By promising to tell her as soon as they arrive at Randalls.

35   Emma walks on in silence and comes to the conclusion that
    A   Mr Weston has disinherited his son.
    B   Mr Weston must have fallen out with someone.
    C   Mrs Weston is expecting a baby.
    D   the family must be having financial problems.

36   Emma enquires after the man on horseback
    A   to distract herself.
    B   out of curiosity.
    C   to take Mr Weston mind off the matter.
    D   because she thought she recognised him.

Part 6

You are going to read an article about the discovery of DNA. Six sentences have been removed from the article. Choose from the sentences **A-G** the one which fits each gap (**37-42**). There is one extra sentence which you do not need to use.

Mark your answers **on the separate answer sheet**.

Crick and Watson and the Discovery of DNA

In 1953, Francis Crick walked into a pub in Cambridge, England and told everyone that he and his colleague, Watson, had found 'the secret of life'. **37** [   ]

The 'Double Helix'

In 1951, Francis Crick was working at the Cavendish Laboratory in the physics department of the University of Cambridge. He was joined there by an American scientist, James Dewey Watson. They had similar scientific interests and started working on the project to uncover the structure of DNA, or deoxyribonucleic acid. **38** [   ] From this new knowledge they then worked out that DNA was the main way that inherited information was passed from parent to offspring in all animals and plants – this was the true 'secret of life'.

The Nobel Prize

It was one of the most significant and important scientific breakthroughs of the last century. The men who first described it, and Maurice Wilkins from the University of London, were awarded the Nobel Prize for Physiology or Medicine in 1962. There are many people who say that these three men would not have been able to make their discovery without the work of Rosalind Franklin also of London University. **39** [   ] However, she died in 1958 and Nobel Prizes are not given posthumously.

What is DNA?

DNA is the chemical substance which chromosomes and genes are made up of. DNA has a structure which looks like a twisting ladder and is made up of pairs of four 'building blocks', called adenine (A), thymine (T), guanine (G) and cytosine (C). **40** [   ]

What is the importance of this discovery today?

Forensic scientists working on a crime use a process called DNA profiling. They use human samples taken from the place where a crime has happened and look at the pattern of pairs A, T, G and C from the DNA. Each of us has a unique pattern, and this means that it is a very reliable way of proving who the criminal is. **41** [   ] This information can be used to match a sample, and hopefully a crime can be solved.

Another important, and sometimes controversial, use of DNA (or rather rDNA which is artificial, or man-made, DNA) is in the areas of biology and biochemistry to produce genetically modified organisms (GMO). **42** [   ]

A   She had developed sophisticated X-ray imaging techniques to 'photograph' DNA.

B   In the UK there is a growing national collection of DNA profiles taken from thousands of people.

C   That dramatic statement must have had quite an effect on the pub's customers that day, and what's more, it was true, and it was going to change completely the way we look at life.

D   The forensic scientists were not able to process the scene of the crime.

E   DNA can make copies of itself, a process called self-replication.

F   DNA-based technology can also be used in anthropology to discover your distant ancestors and how population groups are related across the planet.

G   Using a combination of new mathematical theories, the latest X-ray imaging techniques and some blinding inspiration, they uncovered the now-familiar double helix structure of DNA.

Part 7

You are going to read a magazine article about four different celebrities. For questions **43-52**, choose from the people (**A-D**). The people may be chosen more than once.

Mark your answers **on the separate answer sheet**.

Which person

stumbled upon their career by chance?		43
had a relative who conducted a choir?		44
got their first contract when they were still at school?	45	46
takes their work along with them wherever they may go?		47
had a relative who taught the members of a famous band to play a musical instrument?		48
was chosen for a unique role?		49
didn't follow in their father's footsteps?		50
was asked to perform at a very important occasion?		51
has won many awards but never an Oscar?		52

Star Quality

A

Clive Owen

Clive is the son of a Country and Western singer, Jess Owen. He is the fourth of five brothers, two of whom are musicians. His family were poor and as a child he was not encouraged in this acting talent. Clive didn't let that put him off, he was determined to be a success. He had his first acting role at 13 and then went on to study at the prestigious Royal Academy of Dramatic Art (RADA) in London. Clive eventually became a Hollywood star at the age of forty, after decades as an actor on British TV series and films. George Clooney describes him as 'the greatest discovery of recent times.' Although Clive says no one spoke to him about it, many people thought he would be the next James Bond after Pierce Brosnan, in the end, of course, that job went to Daniel Craig. Clive was nominated for an Oscar and has won a number of awards, including the BAFTA and Golden Globe awards.

B

Cate Blanchett

As a child, Cate studies dance and piano. At the age of 18 she goes on holiday to Egypt and gets a walk-on part in an Egyptian film about a boxer. It is this experience that makes her fall in love with acting and she decides that this is the career she wants to follow. She studies at the National Institute of Dramatic Arts in Sydney and starts working in the theatre and in TV serials. She gets her first film role in 1997 and the following year she stars in Shekhar Kapur's *Elizabeth* for which she receives an Oscar nomination. Over the next few years Cate Blanchett stars in some of the most successful films of all time and then in 2004 she appears in Martin Scorsese's *The Aviator* with Leonardo DiCaprio and is awarded an Oscar for Best Supporting Actress. In 2007 she is the only woman chosen to interpret one of six aspects of the life and work of Bob Dylan in the film *I'm Not There* and is awarded the Volpi Cup for Best Actress at the 64th Venice Film Festival.

C

Usher

Usher discovers his talent for singing at an early age. He joins his local gospel choir in his home town in Tennessee, where his mother is the conductor. He signs a record deal while he is still at high school. His debut album *Usher* is released in 1994 and one of the singles from the album does so well in the charts that he is asked to sing for the Olympics held in Atlanta in 1996. The release of Usher's album *All About U* is planned for 2001, but the songs are illegally uploaded onto the web which millions of people are able to download for free! His record label abandons the release of that album and Usher begins work on some new tracks. The new album is called *8701* (because that is the album's release date) and is a huge hit. Usher is one of the most successful R&B artists in the world. To date he has sold over 30 million albums and has received 5 Grammy Awards.

D

Norah Jones

Norah Jones has music in her genes! Her father is Ravi Shankar, the Indian maestro who taught the Beatles how to play the sitar. Her mother, Sue Jones, was a dancer and singer of soul music. Her grandmother adores country music and Norah's sister is also a singer. At an early age, Norah joined the school choir, where she learnt how to sing. She began playing the piano at the age of five and briefly played the alto saxophone. She won the Down Beat Student Music Award (SMA) for Best Original Composition in 1996 and for two years running was awarded the SMA for Best Jazz Vocalist. In 2000, a music producer heard some of Norah's work and recognised her great talent. The director of Blue Note, the most important record label in jazz, signed her up that year. When she was 23, she released *Come away with me* which won her 8 Grammy Awards and sold 18 million copies. In 2004, after releasing *Feels like home*, she went on a world tour, taking her guitar and notebooks with her so she could write the songs for her next album *Not too late*, which was released in 2007.

Part 1

You **must** answer this question. Write your answer in **140-190** words in an appropriate style on the separate answer sheet.

1   In your English class you have been talking about communication among teenagers. Now your English teacher has asked you to write an essay for homework.

Write your essay using **all** the notes and giving reasons for your point of view.

Teenagers are more confident talking to each other via smartphones than face-to-face. Do you agree?

Notes
Write about:
1 not having a smartphone
2 friendship
3 ——————— (your own idea)

Part 2

Write an answer to **one** of the questions **2-5** in this part. Write your answer in **140-190** words in an appropriate style on the separate answer sheet. Put the question number in the box at the top of the answer sheet.

2 Your teacher told you a new student from the UK would be joining your class next semester. She/He has asked you to prepare a report for the student about school routine and school facilities.

> Your report should:
> • include information about lessons, meals and afternoon activities
> • recommend which lessons would be more appropriate for English speakers

Write your **report**.

3 You see this announcement on an English-language website:

> ### The most important event in my life
> What has been the most important event in your life? When did it happen?
> What was it about? Why was it so important?
> Write us an article answering these questions.
> The best articles will be posted on our website.

Write your **article**.

4 You have seen this announcement in an international magazine for teenagers:

> ### Stories wanted
> Write a story for our magazine. Your story must **begin** with this sentence:
> *Juliet received a phone call and decided to rush to the hospital immediately.*

Write your **story**.

5 Answer the following question based on the title below.

The Importance of Being Earnest by Oscar Wilde

Your English class has had a discussion about *The Importance of Being Earnest*. Now your teacher has given you this essay for homework:

Which character do you feel most sympathy for?

Write your **essay**.

Part 1

(13) You will hear people talking in eight different situations. For questions **1-8**, choose the best answer (**A**, **B** or **C**).

1   You overhear a woman talking to her son on the phone.

What would she like him to do?
A   stop getting into debt
B   buy better quality clothes
C   get a better paid job

2   You hear a man talking about city life.

What is he complaining about?
A   that he finds it difficult to breath when he goes out
B   that he has to wear a mask when he rides to and from the office
C   that he can't afford to live in the countryside

3   You overhear a man and a woman talking.

What is the woman upset about most?
A   that nobody raised the alarm
B   that her husband could be so forgetful
C   that she had to wait outside in her night wear

4   You hear a teacher reciting the myth of Jason and the Golden Fleece.

How was the Golden Fleece stolen?
A   Hercules and Orpheus gave the dragon a potion to send it to sleep.
B   The Argonauts got it out of the wood and took it back to Greece in the Argo.
C   Jason managed to steal the Fleece while the dragon was sleeping.

5   You hear part of a talk on the radio.

What is the man talking about?
A   a short trip
B   an expert on Shakespeare
C   a play

6   You hear a woman talking about a diet.

What does she say about the diet?
A   It made her feel weak.
B   It left an awful taste in her mouth.
C   She couldn't stick to it.

7   You overhear a man talking about his new job.

What does he do?
A   a doctor
B   a psychologist
C   a salesman

8   You overhear a woman talking to a friend.

What is she doing?
A   complaining about something
B   giving him advice
C   warning him

Part 2

(14) You will hear an expert talking about the mystery surrounding the origins of Stonehenge.
For questions **9-18**, complete the sentences with a word or short phrase.

Stonehenge

Archaeologists have been attempting to find out why Stonehenge was

| 9 | | for centuries.

They have wondered over whether it could have been an area dedicated to | 10 | |

A team of experts believe that the | 11 | | circle of stones originated from as far
away as Wales.

A geomorphologist thought it highly improbable that Bronze Age man had | 12 | |
the stones to Stonehenge.

The *Oxford Journal of Archaeology* made the assumption that the bluestones had been torn away by

| 13 | |

The Cursus are avenues of long ago which | 14 | | the area encircling the stones.

A team of archeologists discovered a particle of an | 15 | |
while excavating an ancient burial site.

The theory that the Cursus might have been a chariot | 16 | | in Roman times was
abandoned when it was found out it dated much further back.

It is thought that the stones were transferred to the middle of the site from the

| 17 | | in 2300 BC.

When Stonehenge was first built, the number of | 18 | | from Wales may have
been as many as fifty-six.

Part 3

(15) You will hear five different people talking about various holiday experiences. For questions **19-23**, choose from the list (**A-H**), what each person says about the holidays. Use the letters only once. There are three extra letters which you do not need to use.

A	An important event might have to be postponed.	Speaker 1	19
B	The tourists were taken in by the travel agency.	Speaker 2	20
C	One of the holiday makers couldn't muster any enthusiasm.	Speaker 3	21
D	The flyer was to prevent people from being swindled.	Speaker 4	22
E	Neither insurance company was willing to cover costs incurred.	Speaker 5	23
F	The customers were unaware that they could get their money back.		
G	They are all willing to repeat the experience.		
H	Holiday rules were crystal clear before its start.		

Part 4

(16) You will hear an interview with a musician about teaching children to play a musical instrument. For questions **24-30**, choose the best answer (**A**, **B** or **C**).

24   Music can be taken up
  A   only by people with good physical coordination.
  B   by people looking for a rewarding pastime.
  C   by anyone wishing to do so.

25   A sure sign of enthusiasm is when children
  A   don't have to be reminded to practise.
  B   choose their favourite instrument to learn to play on.
  C   stop playing around with their instrument and take it more seriously.

26   The recorder is a suitable instrument to start with because
  A   children find it less difficult to blow once they've got their second set of teeth.
  B   it doesn't require as much strength to blow as other woodwind instruments.
  C   children feel more at ease with this instrument than a violin or cello.

27   Starting lessons before the age of eight
  A   can give a child the chance to acquire a taste for music.
  B   can allow a child to learn about different musical instruments.
  C   can be too demanding for a child.

28   Music therapy
  A   is particularly suitable for children who have been ill-treated.
  B   stimulates children and enhances their social skills.
  C   and its impact have been heavily remarked upon.

29   State registered therapists
  A   work in health centres administered by the Government.
  B   are qualified professionals who have successfully completed a training course.
  C   provide training courses at APMT.

30   The ability to express oneself through music
  A   depends on musical expertise.
  B   relies on spoken language.
  C   is an inborn competence.

Good morning/afternoon/evening. My name is ——————— and this is my colleague ———————.

And your names are?

Can I have your mark sheets, please?

Thank you.

First of all we'd like to know something about you.

- Where are you from, (*Candidate A*)?
- And you, (*Candidate B*)?
- What do you like about living (*here / name of candidate's home town*)?
- And what about you, (*Candidate A/B*)?

Select one or more questions from any of the following categories, as appropriate.

Homelife

- Tell me something about your home town. What do you like about it?
- What do you do when you're at home? Who do you spend time with?
- Do you come from a large family? How many brothers and sisters have you got?
- Which is your favourite room in the house? Can you describe it to me?
- Have you ever thought about moving? Where would you move to?

Likes and Dislikes

- What do you like doing in your spare time? Why?
- Do you have any hobbies? How much time do you dedicate to your hobby?
- What's your favourite TV programme? What do you like about it?
- Do you like going to the cinema? Tell us about a film you saw recently.
- Tell us about a holiday you really enjoyed recently.

Holidays and Travel

- What's the most tiring journey you've ever been on? Tell us about it.
- Is public transport reliable where you live? Do you ever use it?
- Have you planned your next holiday yet? Where would you like to go?
- Have you ever lost your passport? How did it happen and what did you do?
- What's the most beautiful place you've ever visited? Can you describe it to us?
- Do you have lots of holiday snaps? Where do you keep them?

1 Friendship **2 Hobbies**	**Part 2** 4 minutes (6 minutes for groups of three)

Interlocutor   In this part of the test, I'm going to give each of you two photographs. I'd like you to talk about your photographs on your own for about a minute, and also to answer a short question about your partner's photographs.

(*Candidate A*), it's your turn first. Here are your photographs. They show **different people enjoying themselves outdoors**.

*Place **Photo 1** in front of Candidate A.*

I'd like you to compare the photographs, and say **how important friendship is to each child**.

All right?

Candidate A
🕐 *1 minute*   _____

Interlocutor   Thank you.

(*Candidate B*), **did you use to have lots of friends when you were a child?**

Candidate B
🕐 *approximately*   _____
30 seconds

Thank you.

Now, (*Candidate B*), here are your photographs. They show **people dedicating time to their hobbies**.

*Place **Photo 2** in front of Candidate B.*

I'd like you to compare the photographs, and say **why you think these hobbies are important to the different people**.

All right?

Candidate B
🕐 *1 minute*   _____

Interlocutor   Thank you.

(*Candidate A*), **which hobby would you rather have and why?**

Candidate A
🕐 *approximately*   _____
30 seconds

Interlocutor   Thank you.

1 (*Candidate A*)

How important is friendship to each of these children?

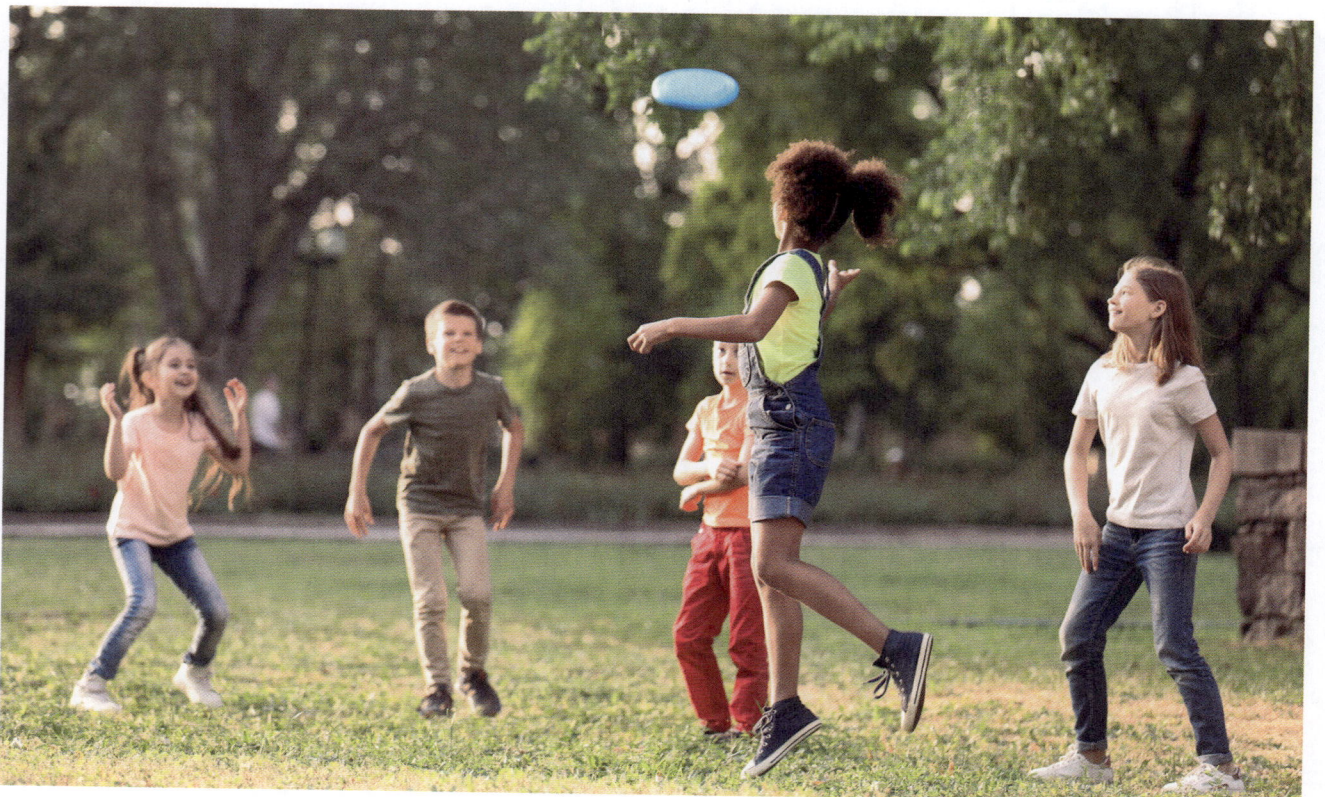

2 (*Candidate B*)

Why are these hobbies important to the different people?

2

21 Education	**Part 3** 4 minutes (5 minutes for groups of three) **Part 4** 4 minutes (6 minutes for groups of three)

Part 3

Interlocutor

Now, I'd like you to talk about something together for about two minutes (*3 minutes for groups of three*).

Here are some reasons why many students prefer studying in groups and a question for you to discuss. First you have some time to look at the task.

(*The interlocutor will show the candidates the page with **Task 21** and will allow 15 seconds.*)

Now, talk to each other about **whether it's a good idea for students to study in groups.**

Candidates
🕐 *2 minutes*
(3 minutes for groups of three)

Interlocutor

Thank you. Now you have about a minute to decide **which two things are the most important for students when they study in groups.**

Candidates
🕐 *1 minute*
(for pairs and groups of three)

Interlocutor

Thank you.

Part 4

Interlocutor

Use the following questions, in order, as appropriate:

- **Do you think group study should be encouraged in schools? Why?**
- **What do you think?**
- **Do you agree?**
- **And you?**
- **If you study in groups, what groups size do you think is best? Why?**
- **What are the advantages of group study? Why?**
- **What are the disadvantages? Why?**
- **Who do you think would benefit most from group study?**

Thank you. That is the end of the test.

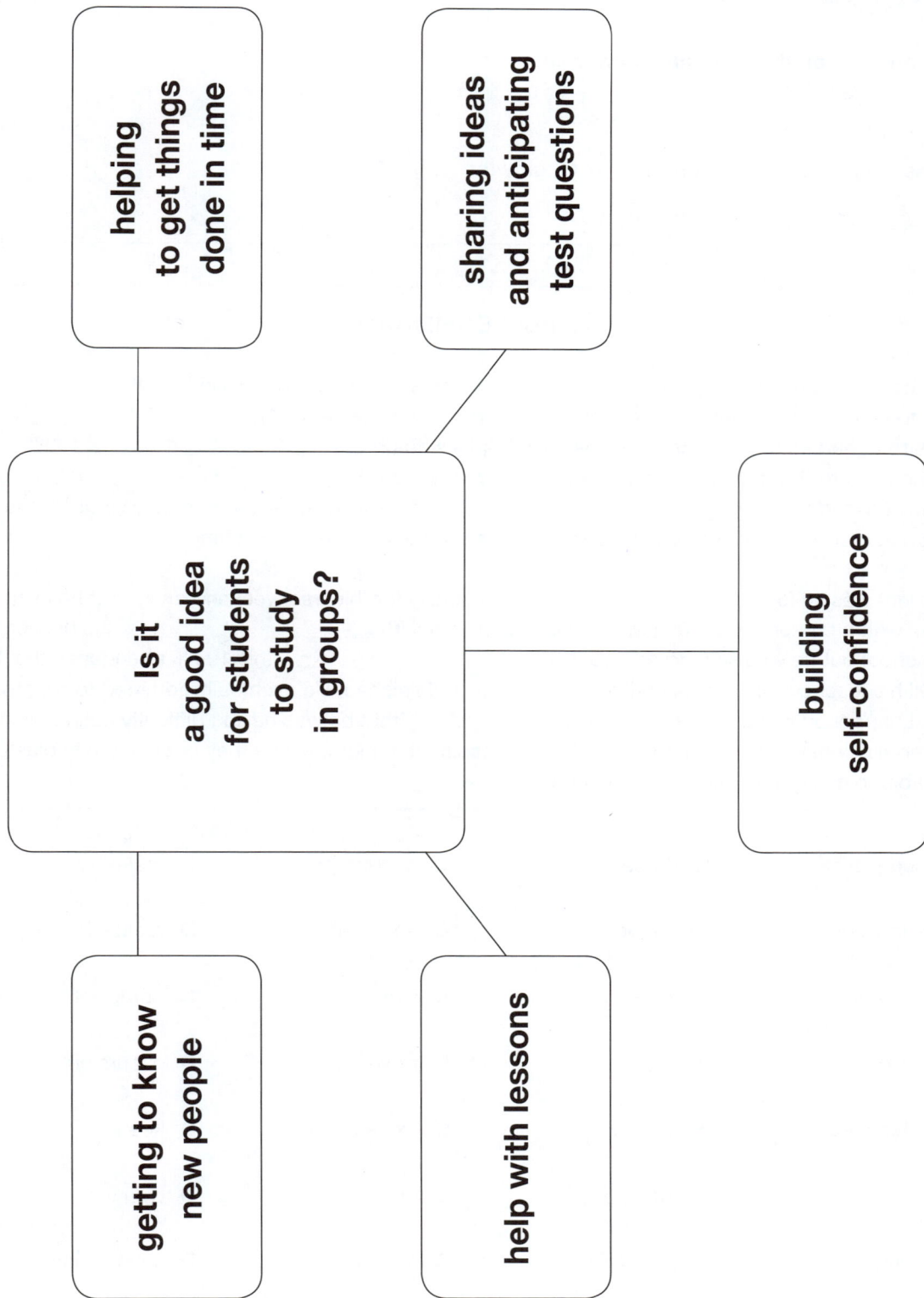

Task 21

helping
to get things
done in time

sharing ideas
and anticipating
test questions

Is it
a good idea
for students
to study
in groups?

building
self-confidence

getting to know
new people

help with lessons

Part 1

For questions **1-8**, read the text below and decide which answer (**A**, **B**, **C** or **D**) best fits each gap.
There is an example at the beginning (**0**).

Mark your answers **on the separate answer sheet**.

Example:

0   **A** serious   **B** important   **C** growth   **D** tragic

0	A	B	C	D
	▬	▭	▭	▭

School Challenges

Truancy has become a (**0**) _____ problem in many schools in recent years. In an attempt to tackle this problem one school introduced a new scheme to (**1**) _____ students to attend as many classes as possible. Pupils who (**2**) _____ a 100% attendance record throughout the whole academic year were (**3**) _____ with an all inclusive weekend school (**4**) _____ to an activity centre where they would be able to have a go at outdoor activities such as climbing, abseiling and white water rafting.

One student was so (**5**) _____ to qualify for this free weekend away that he even went to school with a broken wrist. He hurt his wrist when he fell (**6**) _____ his bike on the way to school but he was so worried about (**7**) _____ his 100% attendance that he didn't tell his teachers or parents until the school day had finished. He eventually admitted to his mother what had happened when she (**8**) _____ that he was having difficulty eating his dinner and asked him what was wrong. She took him to hospital that night, where they put his arm in plaster and he was able to go back to school the next day.

---

1   **A** suggest   **B** force   **C** encourage   **D** make

2   **A** succeeded   **B** made   **C** achieved   **D** realised

3   **A** rewarded   **B** given   **C** won   **D** compensed

4   **A** holiday   **B** trip   **C** travel   **D** excursion

5   **A** interested   **B** happy   **C** excited   **D** keen

6   **A** away   **B** down   **C** off   **D** over

7   **A** filling   **B** maintaining   **C** guarding   **D** succeeding

8   **A** knew   **B** aware   **C** looked   **D** noticed

Part 2

For questions **9-16**, read the text below and think of the word which best fits each gap. Use only **one** word in each gap. There is an example at the beginning (**0**).

Write your answers **IN CAPITAL LETTERS on the separate answer sheet.**

Example: | 0 | | H | A | V | E | | | | | | | | | | | | | | |

Thieves in the safari park

Visitors to Hampton safari park (**0**) _____ been warned not to enter the monkey enclosure (**9**) _____ they have roof cases on their cars as the monkeys (**10**) _____ likely to open them and steal the contents. The animals appear to have worked out a way (**11**) _____ unlocking the cases by jumping on them; they even seem to have been working together in groups to do it.

One family said they knew they couldn't get out of the car and so could only watch in horror (**12**) _____ the monkeys ran away with all their holiday clothes and disappeared up trees with everything from bikinis to shoes. One young monkey (**13**) _____ seen holding onto a child's teddy bear.

Keepers at the safari park said the monkeys had broken into (**14**) _____ than ten roof cases at the beginning of the summer holidays. (**15**) _____ a result they have now set up an alternative route for cars with luggage on the roof (**16**) _____ they can avoid the thieving monkeys.

Part 3

For questions **17-24** read the text below. Use the word given in capitals at the end of some of the lines to form a word that fits in the gap **in the same line**. There is an example at the beginning (**0**).

Write your answers **IN CAPITAL LETTERS on the separate answer sheet.**

Example: | 0 | W E L L - K N O W N

Casablanca

Casablanca is most (**0**) _____ as the title of a classic film   KNOW
from 1942 starring Humphrey Bogart and Ingrid Bergman. But what about the
city where this (**17**) _____ war film was set?   ROMANCE

Casablanca (Spanish for white house), or Casa as it is known by those who
live there, is the largest city in Morocco with a (**18**) _____   POPULATE
of approximately 5 million and is the country's economic capital. Rabat is the
political capital. Casablanca is situated in the west of Morocco on the Atlantic
coast and boasts one of the world's largest artificial ports, a port which was very
(**19**) _____ during the Second World War. At that time   STRATEGY
there was also a large American airbase in Casablanca and in 1943 it was in
Casablanca that a significant conference took place where world
(**20**) _____ met to discuss the progress of the war.   LEAD
Casablanca was (**21**) _____ under the control of the French   FORMAL
from 1910 until 1956 when Morocco gained (**22**) _____.   DEPEND

French influence on the city is (**23**) _____ in the city layout   EVIDENCE
and architecture. French is also the second language after Arabic. The city now
has a growing (**24**) _____ industry, although it is not as   TOUR
popular as other Moroccan cities like Marrakesh and Fez.

Part 4

For questions **25-30**, complete the second sentence so that it has a similar meaning to the first sentence, using the word given. **Do not change the word given**. You must use between **two** and **five** words, including the word given. Here is an example (**0**).

Example:

0   I haven't seen him for at least 2 years.
       TIME
       The _____ was more than 2 years ago.

The gap can be filled by the words 'Last time I saw him', so you write:

Example: | 0 | L | A | S | T | | T | I | M | E | | I | | S | A | W | | H | I | M |

Write **only** the missing words **IN CAPITAL LETTERS on the separate answer sheet.**

25   I won't be satisfied until I have the letter in my possession.
       ONLY
       I will _____ the letter is in my possession.

26   Please tell me as soon as he arrives.
       KNOW
       Please _____ as he arrives.

27   'You're going to be famous one day,' he said to the girl.
       WAS
       He _____ going to be famous one day.

28   There were more spectators than ever before.
       SO
       There _____ spectators before.

29   Do you mind if I borrow your bike tomorrow?
       ME
       Would _____ your bike tomorrow?

30   We can go out for a walk tomorrow if it doesn't rain all day.
       RAINS
       We can go out for a walk tomorrow _____ all day.

Part 5

You are going to read an extract from a novel. For questions **31-36**, choose the answer (**A**, **B**, **C** or **D**) which you think fits best according to the text.

Mark your answers **on the separate answer sheet**.

Being a Pianist

I started playing the piano when I was four years old. My mother thought it would be a good outlet for positive childish energy and I was really into it; it was exciting. It was something different and I had much
5 more time to practise then. The first time I performed in front of an audience was when I was five years old and I loved it. I went on a summer camp run by my piano teachers at the time and at the end of the week we all got up and played a piece. At that age I was unaware
10 of any of the pressure associated with performing live so it just felt nice to have people concentrating on my playing and I liked the applause and attention. Now I perform regularly, often in front of large audiences, and I still really enjoy it.

15 I always knew I wanted to be a pianist and never thought I would do anything else. In that respect I felt different from my friends when I went to school; they all thought they wanted to become teachers or doctors and things like that and I just knew I would be a pianist but it didn't
20 feel strange. Finding time to play and practise wasn't a problem at school until my last few years when the pressure of exams and things was hard, but generally I would choose to practise instead of doing homework. It always felt like schoolwork got in the way of playing the
25 piano rather than the other way around. Unfortunately I was never given any special allowances or extended deadlines though. After I finished school I went on to study a degree in music and now I'm studying a Masters degree in accompaniment.

30 A typical day now involves a couple of hours practice in the morning before going into college and attending classes. I spend a lot of time in the library listening to music, trying to learn and become familiar with new pieces of music. One downside to
35 choosing to study and pursue a career in music

is that you end up spending hours and hours by yourself. However, I also try to spend time at college meeting other people and networking. The more musicians I know the more likely I am to be asked to play for others. The more I play the better known 40 I become and in the music business it's all about recognition and getting your name out there. It's important to get involved in as many performances as possible and take part in competitions so that as many people as possible see you perform and know who 45 you are. It's a very competitive industry. Ultimately, if I am asked to play and get given a job it means that someone else loses work and sometimes it feels like a constant battle. You can't help being drawn into an artificial world where you are constantly comparing 50 yourself to others and are always worried about what others think of your performances. In the real world outside of college your audience is much wider.

I chose to get involved in accompaniment because as much as I love playing the piano I also enjoy 55 working with others. And working as an accompanist is a good way of doing that. There are also more job opportunities as although there is still a lot of competition other performers will always need good accompanists, so there is more demand. I really enjoy 60 performing with other people because there's an even greater sense of achievement when you are both on form and a piece comes out amazingly.

To follow a career in music you have to have a real passion for it as unfortunately it's not a very secure 65 path and it's not usually very well paid. Having said that, the real positive side is that I am doing something I love; it's not just a subject to study. I love everything associated with music and performing and it's what I do every day. 70

31 How did Berrak feel about playing the piano when she was very young?

    A She really enjoyed it.

    B She only did it because her mother wanted her to.

    C She didn't like the fact she had to practice a lot.

    D She felt strange and different from her friends.

32 Why did Berrak feel different from her friends when she was at school?

    A Because the teachers gave her less homework.

    B Because her friends didn't know what career they wanted to follow.

    C Because she was the only one who wanted to become a musician.

    D Because she found the pressure of exams less stressful.

33 Why does she say it is important to meet and talk to other musicians at her college?

    A Because the music industry is very sociable and it's important to have lots of friends.

    B Because she feels lonely after spending so much time by herself.

    C Because other musicians in the college are very supportive of each other.

    D Because it increases her possibilities of being asked to perform.

34 When she says in lines 41-42 that 'in the music business it's all about recognition and getting your name out there' what does she mean?

    A It's important that people know who she is when they see her photograph.

    B It's important that lots of people know what she does and know her name.

    C Her name is more important than the way she plays.

    D Her name needs to be easy for people to recognise and remember.

35 Why did Berrak decide to go into accompaniment?

    A Because she thinks it can be more challenging.

    B Because it's better paid.

    C Because she can achieve more and become more well-known.

    D Because she likes working as part of a team.

36 What does she say is the best thing about studying and pursuing a career in music?

    A She could become rich and famous.

    B There are lots of job opportunities.

    C She spends all her time doing something she loves.

    D She finds it an easy subject.

Part 6

You are going to read an article by retired lawyer and keen cook John Griffiths. Six sentences have been removed from the article. Choose from the sentences **A-G** the one which fits each gap (**37-42**). There is one extra sentence which you do not need to use.

Mark your answers **on the separate answer sheet**.

Cooking for friends

Choosing the degree I should study for at university was quite difficult for me as there were two careers that I found equally attractive: the law and catering. After much soul searching, I realised that whilst I could be a lawyer during the day and then enjoy cookery as a form of relaxation, the reverse was not true. Thus, I opted for a law degree and made food and wine my number one hobby.

I have never regretted this decision. Working as a lawyer provided a good living and allowed me enough spare time to indulge myself by enjoying some very fine food and wines at many superb restaurants. **37** A life in catering would have meant that I would always have been working when my friends were playing and vice versa. The hours that have to be worked by chefs are quite ridiculous. They have to arrive at their restaurant by mid-morning, at the latest, to prepare for lunch. They work all afternoon dealing with the business side of their establishment and developing new recipes. Then, they must prepare for evening service probably crawling into bed in the small hours of the next morning feeling absolutely shattered! **38**

Sharing my love of fine food and wines with good friends in the relaxed atmosphere of my home has more than compensated for not owning a restaurant. **39** Being a professional chef probably would have meant that, by now, I would be sick of the sight of food, much as I am completely turned off by the merest mention of anything to do with the law!

Planning a meal for people I love is a great pleasure. I have a vast collection of cookery books and I am an avid fan of many a TV chef. The problem I have, therefore, is choosing what to cook from so many different possibilities. How do I choose? Well, that depends very much on the friends. A starting point has to be catering for their own likes and dislikes and trying to avoid serving them the same dishes

as last time they visited. **40** I don't claim to be anything other than an enthusiastic amateur but quite a few friends appear to be daunted by the prospect of cooking for me. They seem to think that some of the food I produce is better than they can do and, not wanting to appear to be a show-off or to overwhelm them, I sometimes hold back and cook something simpler than the more adventurous fare I might really have wanted to try.

The friends I like cooking for most of all are those who share the love of food and wine as much as I do and who are quite happy to reciprocate, in grand style, when I pay them a return visit. **41**

Generally, my cooking has become less complex and pretentious over the years and, although I use recipe books and TV chefs as inspiration, I tend to find that the best way of deciding what to cook is to see what is available when I do the shopping. What I cook is controlled by what I have been able to buy. **42** I might have had one or two vague ideas but, more often than not, I am scrabbling through pages of recipes trying to find something new to do with some scallops, a leg of lamb and a punnet of raspberries. I nearly always buy some crème fraiche, a bunch of coriander and some seasonal vegetables. My store cupboard is pretty good and I can usually find all the spices I need, together with onions, garlic, chillies and boring stuff like flour, butter and so on. I strongly believe that if you have good ingredients you will be able to turn out something worth eating.

At the end of a meal there is nothing better than settling down with a strong espresso and a dish of the very best chocolates. The very best of friends can normally provide entertaining conversation but, to me, the finest compliment I can be paid is that they aren't afraid of gently nodding off. It shows that they feel satisfied, relaxed and happy as a result of my efforts!

A   How do you fit a decent social life into that sort of existence?

B   The choices I make depend not only on the wines that might best complement the food but also upon the preferences of my guests.

C   However, it was the luxury of having the time to cook for friends at home that underlined the good sense of the decision I had made.

D   Another factor is their attitude to their own cooking skills.

E   It is one of the great joys of my life and cooking has remained fun.

F   This means that, very often, I don't know what I am giving my friends until a few hours before they arrive.

G   For these friends, I like to pull out all the stops!

Part 7

You are going to read a magazine article about four different campers. For questions **43-52**, choose from the people (**A-D**). The people may be chosen more than once.

Mark your answers **on the separate answer sheet**.

Which person or people:

likes being in the open air surrounded by wildlife?	43
gives an example of people working together to solve a difficult situation?	44
doesn't want to meet the people he/she works with when on holiday?	45
mentions something you can't do on campsites?	46
has enjoyed camping for many years?	47
likes to make last-minute decisions about where to go on holiday?	48
talks about making friends while staying at campsites?	49 50
has been to the same campsite more than once?	51
sees price as a main priority?	52

The Joys of Camping

Camping has been a popular choice for holiday accommodation for a long time but it seems that now its popularity is on the increase. Kate Reilly speaks to 4 dedicated campers and finds out why they prefer to pitch their tents or park their camper vans rather than stay in hotels or rent apartments.

A

Ben: a teacher

For Ben the most important thing is to find a cheap and affordable option during the busy school holidays. 'Because I have to go away during the peak season when all the schools are on holiday it's often difficult to find cheap hotel deals or holiday flats for rent,' he explains. In addition to this he enjoys the flexibility camping offers. 'I'm not that good at planning ahead and like to be spontaneous with my travel plans. The fact that it's not usually necessary to pre-book to stay at a campsite suits me very well. I also like that I can go away to more obscure and remote places and get away from the students I spend all year in the classroom with.

B

Eli and Catriona: doctor and medical researcher

Eli and Catriona explain why camping is the perfect holiday for families. 'We used to go camping when we were much younger, before we had children and loved it but now we have the boys it makes even more sense. There are so many child-friendly campsites with swimming pools and special activities for kids. It's so nice for them to have lots of space to run around in and other children to play with. It also means we have time to ourselves to really relax. We've actually been to the same campsite for 2 years in a row now as we all had such a good time there the first year. The boys are still in touch with friends they made there last year so we might well go back again this year too.'

C

Cathy: finance director

Cathy is looking for a contrast from her stressful working life when she goes on holiday. She says, 'I love being outside and the freedom camping offers. I spend all day in the office when I'm at work and have to be very organised to meet tight deadlines, so when I'm on holiday I like to be in the fresh air and be able to do exactly what I want when I want; camping is perfect for that. Of course there are some rules you have to respect like you're not allowed to make noise after 11 or 12 at night but I like that. I love going to sleep listening to the insects in the trees or the waves on the beach.'

D

Melissa and Stefano: salon manager and marketing director

For Melissa and Stefano it's the friendly atmosphere that means they keep going back to campsites year after year. 'We've travelled around the whole of Europe in our camper van and every year we meet so many interesting people and make friends with people from all over the world.

Everyone is always so helpful when you stay on a campsite. If you need to borrow something like matches your neighbours will always help you out.

One year we got the back wheels of the camper van stuck in the sand and it took ten of our new neighbours to help push it out. Everyone came rushing over to help as soon as they saw there was a problem and most of us didn't even speak the same language. It was a wonderful feeling; you don't get that in hotels.'

Part 1

You **must** answer this question. Write your answer in **140-190** words in an appropriate style on the separate answer sheet.

1   In your English class you have been talking about the importance of getting a good night's sleep. Now your teacher has asked you to write an essay.

     Write your essay using **all** the notes and giving reasons for your point of view.

     Sleep deprivation is a serious problem among teenagers. Do you agree?

     Notes
     Write about:
     1 health
     2 emotional effects
     3 _____ (your own idea)

Part 2

Write an answer to **one** of the questions **2-5** in this part. Write your answer in **140-190** words in an appropriate style on the separate answer sheet. Put the question number in the box at the top of the answer sheet.

2   You have seen this announcement in an international student magazine.

> ## My favourite city
> We're looking for contributors to tell us about their favourite city and tell us about why they like it.
> We will publish the best articles in our next issue.

Write your **article**.

3   You recently saw this announcement in an English language entertainment magazine.

> We are looking for critics to help judge this year's National Drama Award. To enter the competition, you should submit a 140-190-word review of a recent film or play that you have seen. The winning entrants will attend the Monaco Arts Festival at our expense and join a team of professional judges in assessing the Festival productions on stage and screen. Their reviews will also be published in the next issue of *Hot Entertainment Magazine*.

Write your **review**.

4   Your teacher has asked you to write a story for the school magazine. The story must **begin** with the following words:

> *When Jackie eventually looked up she couldn't believe who she saw standing in front of her.*

Write your **story**.

5   Answer the following question based on the title below.

> *The Phantom of the Opera* by Gaston Leroux

Your English class has had a discussion about *The Phantom of the Opera*. Now your teacher has given you this essay for homework:

Which character do you feel most sympathy for? Write an essay giving your opinion and explaining why.

Write your **essay**.

Part 1

(17) You will hear people talking in eight different situations. For questions **1-8**, choose the best answer (**A**, **B** or **C**).

1   You hear a woman talking about her job.

How does she feel about it?
A   It's boring.
B   She likes it.
C   She finds it difficult.

2   You overhear a man telling a friend about a film he saw recently.

What type of film was it?
A   a romance
B   an action film
C   science fiction

3   You hear a man telling his colleague about his holiday.

What was the problem with it?
A   He became ill.
B   He argued with his partner.
C   He couldn't see all the things he wanted to see.

4   You overhear a conversation in a supermarket.

What are they discussing?
A   returning an item
B   breaking an item
C   buying an item

5   You hear an advertisement on the radio.

What is being advertised?
A   a festival
B   a new music album
C   a cake

6   You overhear a woman talking on the phone about her new boss.

What is she worried about?
A   losing her job
B   being given extra work to do
C   her boss is inexperienced

7   You hear an actor talking on the radio about his new film.

What does he say about preparing for the role?
A   He had to learn a new skill.
B   He did lots of research.
C   It was physically challenging.

8   You overhear two people talking about a car.

Why are they talking about the car?
A   It's the man's first car.
B   It's a brand new car.
C   It has broken down.

Part 2

(18) You will hear a talk about an endangered species. For questions **9-18**, complete the sentences with a word or short phrase.

The Iberian Lynx

The Iberian lynx is also known as | 9 |

The Smilodon, or Sabre Toothed Tiger became extinct | 10 |

In recent years the number of Iberian lynx has fallen by | 11 |

Male Iberian lynx can weigh up to | 12 |

The main part of an Iberian lynx's diet consists of | 13 |

During bad weather the Iberian lynx will stay in | 14 |

Due to a change in the law it is no longer legal | 15 |

A female Iberian lynx will be pregnant for a period of | 16 |

Since 2005 | 17 | have been born in the Doñana Breeding Centre.

The World Wildlife Foundation has repeatedly asked the Spanish government
| 18 | which goes through the national park.

Part 3

(19) You will hear five different people talking about holidays they have had. For questions **19-23**, choose from the list (**A-H**), what each person says about the holidays. Use the letters only once. There are three extra letters which you do not need to use.

A	spent a long time planning the holiday.	Speaker 1	19
B	regrets spending a lot of money.	Speaker 2	20
C	was disappointed with the hotel.	Speaker 3	21
D	had an accident during the holiday.	Speaker 4	22
E	enjoyed a very luxurious hotel.	Speaker 5	23
F	went somewhere interesting.		
G	searched for a cheap accommodation.		
H	had a very long holiday.		

Part 4

(20) You will hear an interview with a member of a sporting association. For questions **24-30**, choose the best answer (**A**, **B** or **C**).

24 Where does the sport originate?
   A   South Africa
   B   Britain
   C   Ireland

25 What does he say about the ball?
   A   It's made from leather.
   B   It's made from wood.
   C   It's the same as a tennis ball.

26 How many points is a goal worth?
   A   three
   B   two
   C   one

27 How many kilometres an hour can the ball travel?
   A   115
   B   150
   C   110

28 One of the rules of the game is that you
   A   cannot hold the ball in your hand.
   B   can only carry the ball using the hurley.
   C   must use the hurley to pick the ball up from the ground.

29 What does Sean say about the best hurling players?
   A   They earn too much money.
   B   They earn no money.
   C   They aren't as skilful as they were in the past.

30 What does he say about the fans of the game?
   A   They are aggressive.
   B   Rival fans sit together.
   C   They come from the nobility.

Part 1
2 minutes (3 minutes for groups of three)

Good morning/afternoon/evening. My name is _____ and this is my colleague _____ .

And your names are?

Can I have your mark sheets, please?

Thank you.

First of all we'd like to know something about you.

- Where are you from, (*Candidate A*)?
- And you, (*Candidate B*)?
- What do you like about living (*here / name of candidate's home town*)?
- And what about you, (*Candidate A/B*)?

Select one or more questions from any of the following categories, as appropriate.

Free time and interests

- What do you like doing at weekends?
- Do you prefer to spend your free time alone or with friends? Why?
- How much of your free time do you spend with your family? What sorts of things do you do together?
- Do you have any hobbies that you've done for a long time? What?
- Do you enjoy trying new activities? Have you tried anything new recently?

Daily routine

- Do you prefer getting up early in the morning or staying up late at night? Why?
- What's your favourite day of the week? Why?
- Do you spend a lot of time at home? What do you do there?
- Do you prefer to have the same routine every day or do you prefer to do different things every day? Why?
- Is there anything you'd like to change about your daily routine?

Future plans

- What are you planning to do for your next holiday?
- Is there anything you'd like to study in the future? (What? Why?)
- What job would you like to be doing in 10 years' time?
- Would you like to live abroad in the future?
- Is there anything you're really looking forward to in the next few weeks? (What? Why?)

1 Leisure time 2 Means of transportation	**Part 2** 4 minutes (6 minutes for groups of three)

Interlocutor

In this part of the test, I'm going to give each of you two photographs. I'd like you to talk about your photographs on your own for about a minute, and also to answer a short question about your partner's photographs.

(*Candidate A*), it's your turn first. Here are your photographs. They show **people relaxing in these places**.

*Place **Photo 1** in front of Candidate A.*

I'd like you to compare the photographs, and say **why do you think the people are relaxing in these places**.

All right?

Candidate A
🕐 *1 minute*

Interlocutor

Thank you.

(*Candidate B*), **where do you like to go to relax? Why?**

Candidate B
🕐 *approximately 30 seconds*

Interlocutor

Thank you.

Now, (*Candidate B*), here are your photographs. They show **people and cars**.

*Place **Photo 2** in front of Candidate B.*

I'd like you to compare the photographs, and say **how important you think the cars are to these people**.

All right?

Candidate B
🕐 *1 minute*

Interlocutor

Thank you.

(*Candidate A*), **do you enjoy travelling by car? Why?**

Candidate A
🕐 *approximately 30 seconds*

Interlocutor

Thank you.

1 (*Candidate A*)

Why do you think the people are relaxing in these places?

1

2 (*Candidate B*)

How important do you think the cars are to these people?

2

21 Sports	**Part 3** 4 minutes (5 minutes for groups of three)
	Part 4 4 minutes (6 minutes for groups of three)

Part 3

Interlocutor   Now, I'd like you to talk about something together for about two minutes (*3 minutes for groups of three*).

A university wants to encourage students to do more sports and exercise. Here are some ideas and a question for you to discuss. First you have some time to look at the task.

(*The interlocutor will show the candidates the page with* **Task 21** *and will allow 15 seconds.*)

Now, talk to each other about **why students might like to do each of these sports.**

Candidates
⏱ *2 minutes*
(3 minutes for groups of three)

Interlocutor   Thank you. Now you have about a minute to decide **which two sports would be most popular with students.**

Candidates B
⏱ *1 minute*
(for pairs and groups of three)

Part 4

Interlocutor   Use the following questions, in order, as appropriate:

- **Did you / Would you do any sports like these when you were / are at university? Which ones?**
- **Do you think it's important for students at university to do sports? Why? / Why not?**
- **Do you think young people do enough sport these days?**
- **Whose responsibility is it to make sure young people do enough exercise?**
- **What could governments do to encourage young people to do more sport and exercise?**
- **Is it better for young people to do team sports or individual sports? Why?**
- **When you play a sport does it matter if you win or lose? Why? / Why not?**

Thank you. That is the end of the test.

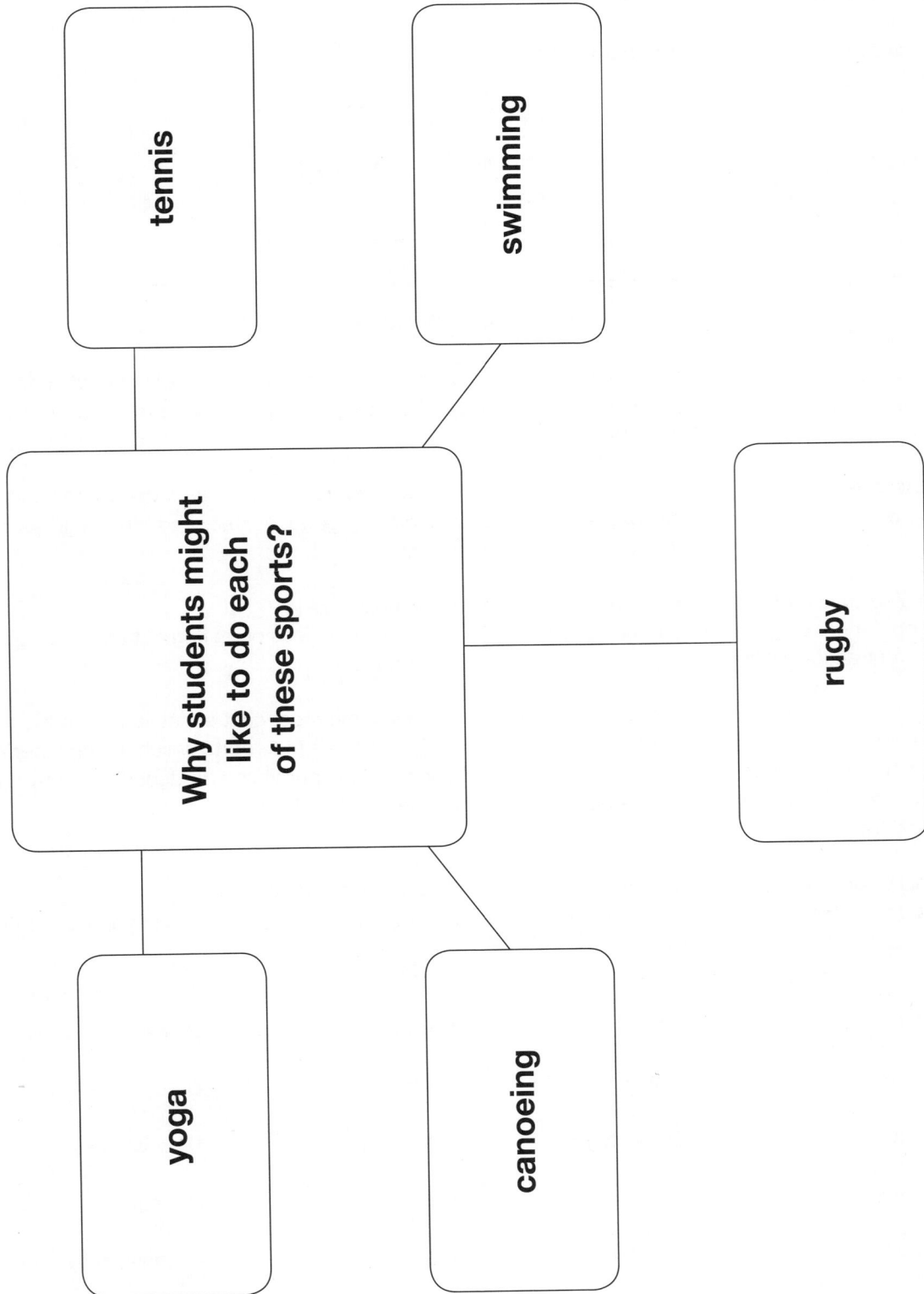

Task 21

tennis

swimming

Why students might like to do each of these sports?

rugby

yoga

canoeing

Part 1

For questions **1-8**, read the text below and decide which answer (**A, B, C** or **D**) best fits each gap. There is an example at the beginning (**0**).

Mark your answers **on the separate answer sheet**.

Example:

0   **A** save   **B** keep   **C** growth   **D** guard

0	A	B	C	D
	▬	▭	▭	▭

Cheaper holidays

We can (**0**) _____ money on all aspects of our holiday, from where and when to go to how to get to and from the airport; here are some tips on how to get the most for your money when (**1**) _____ a holiday.

For the best deals (**2**) _____ your holiday between the high and low seasons; you could save up to 70% on some holiday resorts while still enjoying good weather and other high season (**3**) _____ and there will be fewer crowds.

You can also save money by going somewhere where living costs are (**4**) _____. It might cost more to get there but once you are there you will spend less on eating out and getting around as food and transport will be (**5**) _____ cheaper.

And start saving before you even leave the country by choosing the most cost effective way to the airport. There are many bus services from (**6**) _____ cities to airports which are cheaper than trains. If you go by train book well in advance to get cheaper tickets and if you do decide to go by car, book your carparking as soon as possible; some airports offer up to 50% (**7**) _____ for early bookings.

Finally, make sure you research all the available options on-line. Signing up to email (**8**) _____ can be a good idea as then you will be the first to know about cheap offers. The earlier you book the better the bargains are likely to be.

---

1   **A** deciding   **B** choosing   **C** agreeing   **D** electing

2   **A** book   **B** ask for   **C** order   **D** buy

3   **A** pros   **B** advantages   **C** favours   **D** drawbacks

4   **A** lower   **B** smaller   **C** poorer   **D** greater

5   **A** largely   **B** obviously   **C** quite   **D** significantly

6   **A** main   **B** important   **C** great   **D** major

7   **A** under   **B** below   **C** off   **D** over

8   **A** alarms   **B** warnings   **C** news   **D** alerts

Part 2

For questions **9-16**, read the text below and think of the word which best fits each gap. Use only **one** word in each gap. There is an example at the beginning (**0**).

Write your answers **IN CAPITAL LETTERS on the separate answer sheet**.

Example: | 0 | | O | F | | | | | | | | | | | | | | | | | |

A shorter presentation

Do you find the idea (**0**) _____ sitting through yet another slide show presentation fills you with dread? Do you find (**9**) _____ hard to stay awake when confronted with slide after slide and (**10**) _____ hour-long talk? Well, don't worry, here is a solution. Presentations can be short, attention grabbing and even a competitive sport.

In Japan in 2003 Astrid Klein and Mark Dytham (**11**) _____ looking for a better way for ambitious young architects to show (**12**) _____ work easily, efficiently and informally. They came up with something called Pecha Kucha; a presentation format (**13**) _____ permits only 20 slides and only 20 seconds to talk about (**14**) _____ one. This means the whole presentation lasts exactly 6 minutes and 40 seconds. (**15**) _____ you start with the first slide there is no stopping and no going back.

Pecha Kucha events now take place throughout the world and are immensely popular. The Pecha Kucha format is now being used in (**16**) _____ types of settings including business and academia in cities as far apart as Auckland and Vancouver. So why not try it next time you have to give a presentation?

Part 3

For questions **17-24**, read the text below. Use the word given in capitals at the end of some of the lines to form a word that fits in the gap **in the same line**. There is an example at the beginning (**0**).

Write your answers **IN CAPITAL LETTERS on the separate answer sheet**.

Example: | 0 | F | R | O | Z | E | N | | | | | | | | | | | |

Smoothies

Smoothies are cold drinks made from blended fruit and vegetables to which
crushed ice, milk, honey or (**0**) _____ yoghurt is also often   **FREEZE**
added. This gives them a thicker milkshake-like consistency.
They have long been a popular (**17**) _____ to fizzy drinks and   **ALTERNATE**
are marketed as a healthy option. For many years now they have been
(**18**) _____ available in high street coffee shops and   **WIDE**
supermarkets. They are packed with fruit and vegetables, but are smoothies
really good for us?

One popular brand (**19**) _____ that their drinks contained   **ADVERT**
two of the suggested five portions of fresh fruit or vegetables which we should
consume every day. This claim resulted in an investigation into just how healthy
these drinks really are. The results were good news for all smoothie
(**20**) _____. The research found that the brand's 250ml   **LOVE**
non-dairy drinks did in fact contain sufficient pulped fruit and fruit juice to count
for two of the recommended (**21**) _____ portions of fruit and   **DAY**
vegetables. As a result health officials have agreed that smoothies are good
for us. However, not all smoothies are the same. There is a great diversity of
ingredients and (**22**) _____ are advised to check the contents   **CONSUME**
carefully. Some may contain as much as a quarter of your recommended daily
(**23**) _____ of saturated fat and up to 40g of sugar.   **ALLOW**

In conclusion, it seems that although smoothies are a good source of the
vitamins and minerals found in fruit and vegetables there are also a lot of
(**24**) _____ variations.   **HEALTH**

Part 4

For questions **25-30**, complete the second sentence so that it has a similar meaning to the first sentence, using the word given. **Do not change the word given**. You must use between **two** and **five** words, including the word given. Here is an example (**0**).

Example:

0   I haven't seen him for at least 2 years.
      TIME
      The _____ was more than 2 years ago.

The gap can be filled by the words 'last time I saw him', so you write:

Example: | 0 | L | A | S | T | | T | I | M | E | | I | | S | A | W | | H | I | M |

Write **only** the missing words **IN CAPITAL LETTERS on the separate answer sheet**.

25   I'm sorry, but I disagree with everything you just said.

       NOT

       I'm sorry, but I _____ you just said.

26   I think I'd rather stay at home than go to the party.

       TO

       I think _____ at home tonight.

27   Do I really need to have the operation?

       FOR

       Is it really _____ to have the operation?

28   It was very careless of you to lose my helmet.

       MORE

       You should _____ my helmet.

29   Neil's always forgetting where he has left his keys.

       NEVER

       Neil can _____ he has left his keys.

30   The weather was better than I'd expected.

       BAD

       The weather was _____ I'd expected.

Part 5

You are going to read an extract from a novel. For questions **31-36**, choose the answer (**A**, **B**, **C** or **D**) which you think fits best according to the text.

Mark your answers **on the separate answer sheet**.

Lost Dog

Emily woke up before her alarm went off and knew instantly something wasn't quite right in the house. Bailey, her chocolate-coloured pet Labrador, should have been there at the bedroom door demanding food
5 but there was no sound of him. She decided to get up and go and see where he was. It felt cold in the hall but she knew she had left the heating on last night. As she walked down the stairs she heard a noise in the kitchen; the strange feeling that something was wrong
10 was getting stronger. What was going on? She got to the bottom of the stairs and opened the door to the living room, which led to the kitchen. Why was the door closed? She always left it open. Bailey was nowhere to be seen and his toys, which were usually all over the
15 living room floor, were in a neat pile in the corner next to his basket. Had they been there when she had gone to bed last night? She couldn't remember.

She walked into the kitchen and turned the light on, it didn't work, nothing happened. She stood very still and
20 listened, nothing. There wasn't a sound. That was really strange; she lived in the middle of a busy city, there were always people around. She woke up to the sound of traffic, car horns, police cars, her neighbours shouting in the house next door, how could there be silence at
25 8 o'clock on a Friday morning? She went back into the living room and turned the TV on, but again nothing happened. She went back into the kitchen and looked out of the window; it was a bright clear day. The back door was shut but when she tried the handle she realised
30 it was unlocked.

She walked out into the tiny back garden and opened the back gate; still nothing, not a sound and no sign of Bailey. She called him but he didn't come. She went back into the house and did what she realised she
35 should have done as soon as she got up and called her mother. But there was no answer. She called her boyfriend but his mobile was switched off and she got the answer phone message. She tried a couple of other numbers but with equal success.

She sat down on the sofa and thought about what she 40 could do. She couldn't decide if she should stay at home or go out and find someone. Just as she decided the best thing would be to stay at home and wait, there was a loud banging on the front door. She jumped up and ran to the door. 'Who is it?' she shouted through 45 the door. 'It's me,' came the reply. But she had no idea who 'me' was. She didn't want to open the door until she was sure she knew who it was, not with all the other strange things that were happening this morning, and she didn't want to shout through the thick front door, so 50 she walked back into the living room and tried to look through the front window to see who was standing at the front door. It was a man but she couldn't make out who he was; he didn't look familiar. He was tall and was wearing a big coat with a hood over his head. Just as 55 she was thinking of running out the back door she saw that the man had Bailey with him, and Bailey seemed quite happy, which meant that the man had to be someone he knew and liked; he would have been barking otherwise. She still wasn't taking any chances 60 though; she put the safety latch on the door and opened it just enough to see who was there. She was instantly relieved; it was her brother, who lived just a few streets away. She opened the door all the way and let him in. As he walked through the door he was almost knocked 65 over by Bailey jumping up and looking more pleased than ever to see her.

'So what's going on?' she asked her brother. He looked at her as if she was stupid.
'Haven't you heard?' 70

31   How did Emily know there was something wrong?

    A Her alarm clock didn't go off.

    B Her dog wasn't outside the bedroom door.

    C Her dog was quieter than usual.

    D She had woken up very early.

32   What could she hear when she stood in the kitchen?

    A traffic and everyday noises of the city

    B silence

    C the television

    D something in the garden

33   Why did she go into the garden?

    A to see what the weather was like

    B to talk to her neighbours

    C to look for Bailey

    D to make a phone call

34   Who did she speak to on the telephone?

    A her mother

    B her boyfriend

    C two friends

    D no one

35   Why did she think she must know the man at the door?

    A She recognised the clothes he was wearing.

    B Bailey was barking at him.

    C Bailey seemed relaxed with him.

    D She recognised his voice.

36   What does the author mean in line 60 when it says that 'she still wasn't taking any chances though'?

    A She wasn't feeling lucky.

    B She was going to take advantage of the situation.

    C She wasn't going to waste the opportunity.

    D She wasn't going to take any risks.

Part 6

You are going to read an article in which stage manager Adam James talks about his work in technical theatre. Six sentences have been removed from the article. Choose from the sentences **A-G** the one which fits each gap (**37-42**). There is one extra sentence which you do not need to use.

Mark your answers **on the separate answer sheet**.

Technical Theatre

I was 12 years old when I first saw a show in my local leisure centre. I was fascinated by the fact that everything came in about ten lorries and they basically built a theatre from scratch. **37** [ ]
I got to know some of the people working on the stage management team and they let me shadow them while they worked. I met the stage manager and after watching the team work and talking to him I decided that was what I wanted to do as a job. I didn't know anything about work in the theatre industry so I started studying and learning about the job. **38** [ ] However, what I really wanted was to get involved and start working as part of a stage management team. Once I was 14 I managed to get some work experience and I started to miss school sometimes and go to work at the theatre instead.

I left school when I was 16 and because I had quite a lot of experience I was able to get a job as an assistant stage manager in a theatre in London. I worked there for about a year and then did some freelance work in Cornwall and went on tours around the country. **39** [ ] Working on tour was intense but really good fun. A typical Monday would see us arrive at about 8 o'clock in the morning and open up the lorries. We would have some coffee and then when everyone had arrived we would spend the day building the show. In the afternoon the cast would arrive and I would show them around so they knew where they could make quick costume changes and things like that. **40** [ ] Once the show had started it was just a case of watching and supervising and letting the show happen around us. As stage manager I was always the first and the last person on stage. Working on tour can be stressful as you have to keep track of where everyone is for health and safety reasons and monitor everything that goes on back stage and keep to time. Then once the show is over you have to check everything and make a note of everything that needs repairing or re-doing before the next performance.

After a couple of years touring I decided to return to London and go to college to study technical theatre. I studied for a year but I realised that it wasn't very useful to me. I had learnt a lot more from my years working. I felt like I was already established in the industry so I decided to leave college and got a job in a theatre. When finding work in technical theatre first-hand experience is much more important than qualifications. **41** [ ] I did some more freelance work in London for a while and now I work for a production company.

You can have up to 20 people working on any one performance so there's a real team spirit. There are people working in lighting, sound, wardrobe, wigs, props, carpentry and stage management. Apart from the technical side we also have to look after the actors. As stage manager it's my job to meet and greet the cast on their first day and make sure they know where everything is and have everything they need. The hardest thing I've ever had to do was try to control 2,500 primary school children. I really like what I do. There are of course a number of disadvantages; I don't like the hours and the disruption to my personal life that working evenings can cause. **42** [ ]
But I would highly recommend it to others; it's very enjoyable and always different; you never have the same day twice and there's something very exciting and beautiful about live theatre.

A   The more I found out about technical theatre the more interested I became.

B   Also there's quite a lot of instability and insecurity to the job and the money is not always good.

C   While the cast were getting ready we would get on with any necessary maintenance jobs.

D   I was very curious as I watched the whole thing being put together and I found it hugely exciting.

E   Working in a large theatre is much more difficult because there are so many more people to organise.

F   The work was quite sporadic but the money was good; in one month I could earn enough to last me six months.

G   Theatres are looking for people with proven ability and who know what they are doing, and what interests them the most on your CV is your last job.

Part 7

You are going to read an article in which four people talk about what they have done to raise money for charity. For questions **43-52**, choose from the people (**A-D**). The people may be chosen more than once.

Mark your answers **on the separate answer sheet**.

Which person or people:

would not repeat what they did to raise money?	43
spent a long time preparing for what they did?	44
says raising money for charity was their secondary aim?	45 46
says the experience was unique and memorable?	47
did their challenge with a group of people?	48 49
had a family member help them with the preparation for the event?	50
took part in the same event many times?	51
didn't enjoy the event as much as the preparation?	52

Raising money for charity

A

Housewife and grandmother

I abseiled off a cliff to raise money for charity. It was an enormous challenge as I'm actually quite afraid of heights. It was only really the moment of going over the edge that was difficult; after that it was very easy. You just have to get into the rhythm and not go too fast. My son is very into climbing and things like that and he and some of his friends from his university climbing club set everything up and organised the whole event. There were about twenty of us who did it and between us we raised well over the target amount. It was a great success but I don't think I'll be doing anything like that again. Once was enough!

B

Environmental consultant

I cycled from L.A. to Quito last spring. All my family thought I was mad but I love cycling and I knew it would be an amazing way to see lots of really interesting places that most people never see. I managed to raise quite a bit of money for charity through sponsorship although that wasn't my main objective. I turned 30 in March and I really wanted to be doing something totally different rather than just sitting at my desk in the office. I wanted it to be different and something I could look back on when I am older and feel proud of. It is something I'll be able to tell my grandchildren about and the fact that I was able to do something to help those less well off than me at the same time, well that made it even better.

C

Lawyer

I ran a triathlon and managed to get over 50 people to sponsor me. I had to train for months and it was really hard work but well worth it. I actually enjoyed the training more than the final event because on the day the weather was terrible. In the months running up to the event I followed a very strict regime and it felt good to be working towards such a specific goal. I would often get up at 5 o'clock in the morning so I could train before going to work. Knowing that I was going to be able to give a large donation to charity made me even more determined to do it. It wasn't compulsory to get sponsorship and giving money to charity wasn't my main motivation when I first signed up to do it but I wanted to make the most of the opportunity and all my friends and family were really supportive and wanted to help and give money. It was such a positive experience I'm going to do it again next year.

D

Theatre manager

When I was a child I took part in a lot of sponsored walks. Each year my school would organise the walks and although it wasn't compulsory my friends and I would always take part. It was fun.

Each walk was about 15 km long so it took quite a long time but it was a nice way to spend a day. The first year I did it I was only 11 years old and my father came with us to keep an eye on us but once we were older we went by ourselves; there were about 8 or 9 of us that all walked together. We managed to get quite a bit of money between us; in fact it became our challenge to raise more money than the year before, which we always achieved, so there was a great sense of satisfaction.

Part 1

You **must** answer this question. Write your answer in **140-190** words in an appropriate style on the separate answer sheet.

1   In your English class you have been talking about money. Now your teacher has asked you to write an essay.

Write your essay using **all** the notes and giving reasons for your point of view.

When choosing a job, the salary is the most important aspect to consider.
To what extent do you agree or disagree?

Notes
Write about:
1 jobs you like / salary
2 importance of money
3 _____ (your own idea)

Part 2

Write an answer to **one** of the questions **2-5** in this part. Write your answer in **140-190** words in an appropriate style on the separate answer sheet. Put the question number in the box at the top of the answer sheet.

2

> The teachers at your school have complained that many students are spending too much time using the Internet to visit social networking sites and chat rooms. They have asked the Head teacher to disconnect the Internet from the school's computer room as they feel it is not an appropriate use of school equipment.
> Write a report to the Head teacher explaining why internet access should be available to the students. Make some suggestions about ways in which internet access can be controlled.

Write your **report**.

3   You have decided to enter a short story competition. The rules of the competition say that you must **begin** with the words:

> *John woke up one morning to see a large hole in the wall where his wardrobe used to be.*

Write your **story**.

4   You have received this email from your English-speaking friend Thea.

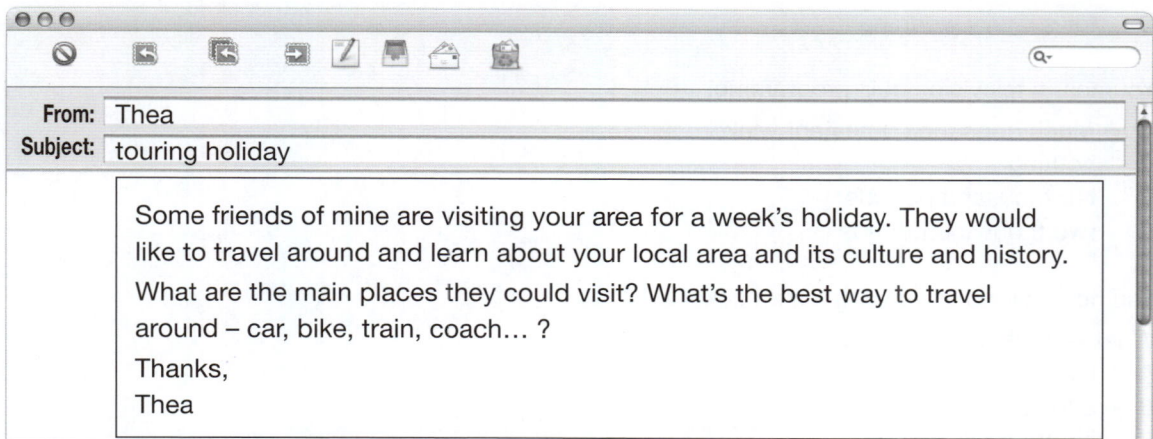

From: Thea
Subject: touring holiday

> Some friends of mine are visiting your area for a week's holiday. They would like to travel around and learn about your local area and its culture and history.
> What are the main places they could visit? What's the best way to travel around – car, bike, train, coach… ?
> Thanks,
> Thea

Write your **email**.

5   You recently saw this notice in a magazine called *The Theatre Goer*.

> When did you last go to the theatre? What did you see and what was it like?
> Write a review and tell us what you thought of the acting and the scenery.
> The most entertaining reviews will win two free tickets to next month's show!

Write your **review**.

Part 1

(21) You will hear people talking in eight different situations. For questions **1-8**, choose the best answer (**A**, **B** or **C**).

1   You hear a woman talking about a young man.

What is her relationship to him?
A   his mother
B   his teacher
C   his neighbour

2   You hear a man talking about a house.

Why did he decide not to buy it?
A   It was too expensive.
B   It wasn't big enough.
C   It was too far away.

3   You hear someone talking about a concert they went to.

How did they feel about the concert?
A   It was too short.
B   She enjoyed it.
C   The music was disappointing.

4   You hear somebody talking about a trip they are about to take.

Why are they going?
A   on business
B   on holiday
C   for a family wedding

5   You hear a television quiz programme.

How much does the contestant win?
A   nothing
B   ten thousand pounds
C   two thousand pounds

6   You hear somebody buying a train ticket.

What kind of ticket do they buy?
A   a single
B   a fixed return
C   an open return

7   You hear a young woman talking about her decision to leave home.

Why did she decide to leave home?
A   because of her relationship with her parents
B   to be nearer to work
C   because she wanted to live with a friend

8   You hear a radio advertisement.

What is it advertising?
A   a soft drink
B   a holiday
C   a pizza restaurant

Part 2

(22) You will hear a radio news item about a hot air balloon manufacturer. For questions **9-18**, complete the sentences with a word or short phrase.

An award for Douglas Finch

Douglas Finch is to be awarded the Honorary Degree of Doctor of [**9**   ]

Douglas Finch was born near Glasgow and attended Allan Glen's School before reading

[**10**   ] at Glasgow University.

The Bristol Belle was the first hot air balloon in [**11**   ]

In 1968 he was issued with the first ever [**12**   ] for Hot Air Balloons.

The Golden Falcon was designed specifically to fly [**13**   ]

In 1973 he was awarded the Royal Aeronautical Club Silver Medal for the first balloon flight

[**14**   ]

In 1978 he attempted to cross the Atlantic in a balloon called [**15**   ]

Bristol is considered the undisputed [**16**   ] of the world.

Doug Finch has advanced the science, technology and art of balloon flight to

[**17**   ]

Doug Finch will receive his Honorary [**18**   ] at Bristol Business School.

Part 3

(23) You will hear five different people talking about the place where they live. For questions **19-23**, choose from the list (**A-H**), what each person feels about where they live. Use the letters only once. There are three extra letters which you do not need to use.

A	hasn't lived there very long.	Speaker 1	19
B	has lots of friends in the area.	Speaker 2	20
C	lives in a very poor area.	Speaker 3	21
D	regrets moving there.	Speaker 4	22
E	is thinking about leaving the area.	Speaker 5	23
F	likes the shops in the area.		
G	thinks the area has become dangerous.		
H	is moving somewhere else.		

Part 4

(24) You will hear an interview with an athlete talking about his sport. For questions **24-30**, choose the best answer (**A**, **B** or **C**).

24   What is the sport called?
  - **A**   Half Marathons
  - **B**   Ultra-Marathons
  - **C**   Fun running

25   The races
  - **A**   are varied.
  - **B**   are timed.
  - **C**   cover a fixed length.

26   How many people compete in the South African race?
  - **A**   12,000
  - **B**   250
  - **C**   200

27   How does Stan feel about the Badwater race?
  - **A**   It's frightening.
  - **B**   It's impossible.
  - **C**   It's a good personal test.

28   When was the first Badwater race completed?
  - **A**   1974
  - **B**   1980
  - **C**   1977

29   How long did it take Al Arnold to finish it?
  - **A**   18 hours
  - **B**   80 hours
  - **C**   49 hours

30   What does Stan say he values most about the sport?
  - **A**   He has come to terms with his temper.
  - **B**   It has made him more responsible.
  - **C**   He realises how grateful he is to have friends and family.

Part 1
2 minutes (3 minutes for groups of three)

Good morning/afternoon/evening. My name is —————— and this is my colleague ——————.

And your names are?

Can I have your mark sheets, please?

Thank you.

First of all we'd like to know something about you.

- Where are you from, (*Candidate A*)?
- And you, (*Candidate B*)?
- What do you like about living (*here / name of candidate's home town*)?
- And what about you, (*Candidate A/B*)?

Select one or more questions from any of the following categories, as appropriate.

Special occasions

- What special occasions do you celebrate?
- Do you normally celebrate them with friends or family? Why?
- Tell us about a festival or celebration in your country.
- How do you celebrate your birthday? What did you do on your last birthday?
- Are you going to do anything special this weekend? (What? Where?)

Media

- How much TV do you watch in a week? What do you usually watch?
- Tell us about a TV programme you particularly like and the reason why.
- Do you use the Internet every day? How many hours a day? What for?
- Do you ever listen to the radio? What programmes do you like? Why?
- Do you usually read newspapers? How often?

Travel and holidays

- Tell us about a special place you've visited.
- Is there anywhere in the world you'd really like to visit? (Where? Why?)
- Do you like to spend your holiday in the same place each year or do you prefer to go somewhere different each year?
- Do you prefer going on holiday in the summer or winter? Why?
- What do you like to do when you're on holiday?

| 1 Special occasions
2 Shopping | Part 2
4 minutes (6 minutes for groups of three) |

Interlocutor   In this part of the test, I'm going to give each of you two photographs. I'd like you to talk about your photographs on your own for about a minute, and also to answer a short question about your partner's photographs.

(*Candidate A*), it's your turn first. Here are your photographs. They show **people celebrating birthdays**.

*Place **Photo 1** in front of Candidate A.*

I'd like you to compare the photographs, and say **how you think the people are feeling**.

All right?

Candidate A
🕐 *1 minute*   _____

Interlocutor   Thank you.

(*Candidate B*), **how do you usually celebrate your birthday?**

Candidate B
🕐 *approximately*   _____
30 seconds

Interlocutor   Thank you.

Now, (*Candidate B*), here are your photographs. They show **people shopping for food in different places**.

*Place **Photo 2** in front of Candidate B.*

I'd like you to compare the photographs, and say **what the advantages and disadvantages are of shopping in these different places**.

All right?

Candidate B
🕐 *1 minute*   _____

Interlocutor   Thank you.

(*Candidate A*), **where do you like to shop for food? Why?**

Candidate A
🕐 *approximately*   _____
30 seconds

Interlocutor   Thank you.

1 (*Candidate A*)

How do you think these people are feeling?

1

2 (*Candidate B*)

What are the advantages and disadvantages of shopping in these different places?

2

21 Technology	**Part 3** 4 minutes (5 minutes for groups of three)
	Part 4 4 minutes (6 minutes for groups of three)

Part 3

Interlocutor

Now, I'd like you to talk about something together for about two minutes (*3 minutes for groups of three*).

A university wants to carry out a survey on technology. Here are some ideas and a questions for you to discuss. First you have some time to look at the task.

(*The interlocutor will show the candidates the page with* **Task 21** *and will allow 15 seconds.*)

Now, talk to each other about **how important these technological devices are in people's everyday lives.**

Candidates

⏱ *2 minutes*
(3 minutes for groups of three)

Interlocutor

Thank you. Now you have about a minute to decide **which two devices it would be most difficult to live without.**

Candidates B

⏱ *1 minute*
(for pairs and groups of three)

Part 4

Interlocutor

Use the following questions, in order, as appropriate:

- **Which of these is most important for you? Why?**
- **What other machines could people not live without?**
- **Do you think people rely too much on machines these days?**
- **Some people say machines make our lives more complicated rather than simpler. What do you think?**
- **Why do you think some people always like to have the latest and best machines?**
- **Sometimes machines don't work properly or break down. What problems can this cause?**
- **Do you think we will have robots in our homes in the future to do all the housework for us? (Do you think this would be a good thing?)**

Thank you. That is the end of the test.

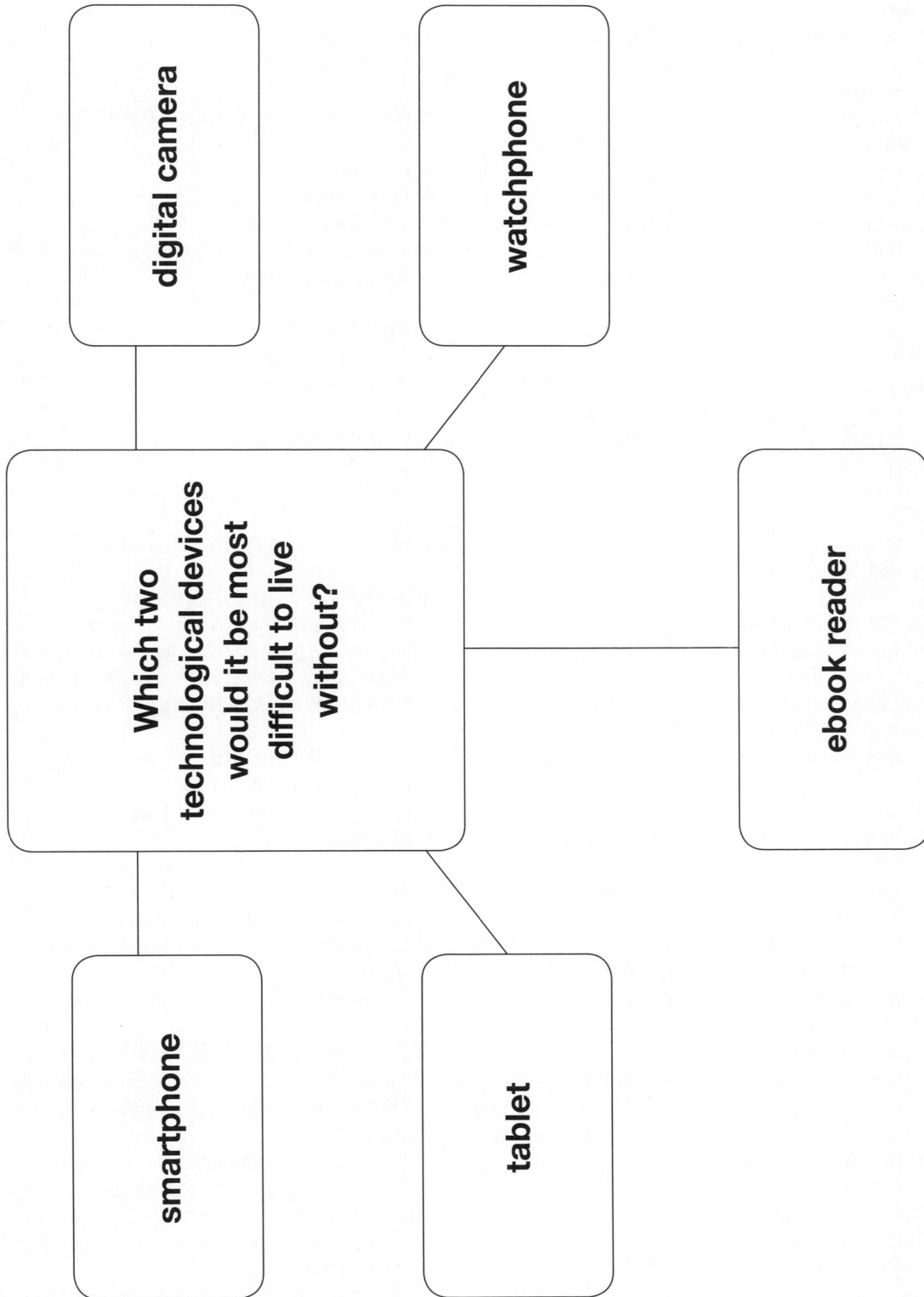

Task 21

digital camera

watchphone

Which two technological devices would it be most difficult to live without?

ebook reader

smartphone

tablet

Writing

Letters objecting to someone's plans
- I am writing to express my concern / disappointment / alarm at hearing...
- I was extremely alarmed / sorry / distressed to hear about your plans to...
- As I think you know...
- May I point out that...
- I feel I really must object to...
- I am extremely concerned at the thought that...
- It must be very clear that...
- I dread to imagine what damage this will cause.
- May I respectfully suggest that you...
- I was wondering if you had considered this alternative.
- Would it not be possible to... ?

Letters of complaint
- I am writing to complain about...
- I am writing to tell you how disappointed / annoyed I feel about...
- I was amazed / distressed / horrified to find that...
- As you must realise, ...
- I am sure you know / you can imagine / you will appreciate that...
- It goes without saying that...
- At the very least, I look forward to receiving...

Letters of recommendation
- I am writing to you on behalf of...
- I have known X for... years.
- She / He has shown herself / himself to be extremely...
- X would seem to fit the requirements of this job perfectly.
- I have no hesitation in recommending X as a...

Letters to the editor
- I am writing about the article on... , which appeared (in last night's paper).
- I am writing with reference to the article you published (in last month's issue).
- I have just read your article on... and I feel I must...
- You raised some issues which I feel strongly about.
- At the start of your article, you appear to claim that...
- I am afraid I totally disagree.
- I am completely in agreement.
- I am sure readers will agree with me when I say that...

Sequencing
- At first / To start with / In the beginning, ...
- Then / Next / After that, ...
- The next thing that happened was ...
- The next thing I knew was ...
- Seconds / Minutes later, ...
- Later on / Some time later, ...
- It wasn't until much later that...
- After some time / After what seemed like years, ...
- Finally / In the end, ...
- At last, ...

Simultaneous events
- Meanwhile / In the meantime, ...
- While all this was going on, ...
- In the middle of all this, ...
- During all this time, ...

Sudden or unexpected events
- Suddenly / All of a sudden, ...
- All at once, ...
- Out of the blue, ...
- Without any warning, ...
- Just when I was least expecting it, ...
- The next thing I knew was...

Rapid events
- As quick as a flash, ...
- In the wink of an eye, ...
- In a matter of seconds / minutes, ...
- In no time at all, ...

Looking back
- In retrospect, ...
- When I think back to what happened then, ...

Introductory comments
- I recently visited (the new Leisure Centre) and have prepared the following report for your consideration.
- Further to my visit to... , I have prepared the following report.
- The following report relates to my recent visit to...

General comments
- On the whole, I found that...
- Although... , I should point out that...
- It is a fact that...

Concluding comments
- All things considered, I believe that...
- Taking all these points into consideration, I would recommend...
- I recommend that we look into the possibility of...

Comparing places or facilities
- One of the main differences between X and Y is that...
- X is completely / entirely / totally different from Y in that...
- Unlike X, Y is...
- While / Whereas / Although X is... , Y is...
- X is a little / slightly / somewhat / a great deal (bigger / more elegant than Y).
- X is not quite / nearly as (comfortable / expensive / convenient) as Y because...
- X is virtually / exactly the same as Y when it comes to...

Proposals
- As requested, I am submitting the following proposal on...
- I recommend that we...
- I propose that we...

- We should also...
- I believe that...
- We could...
- It is a fact that, which means that...
- If we were to, it would...
- I suggest we.... We would then be able to...
- I feel strongly that we should...
- I trust you will give my proposal your full consideration.

Reviews
- X has much to recommend it.
- X is, at heart, a(n) love / spy / adventure story.
- It is based on a book by...
- It is set in the countryside / the future.
- The film has a quality cast.
- The film was directed by...
- The film score is enchanting / evocative / scary.
- The film captures the spirit of...
- The hero / heroine / villain is...
- I felt / thought it was…
- I was impressed by…
- What struck me most was...
- What I liked most / didn't like was...
- The plot was gripping.
- The characters were very convincing / very well drawn.
- On reflection, I think it was...
- It struck me as being...
- What I didn't understand was how...
- In spite of these few criticisms, I think...
- I would have no hesitation in recommending…

Expressing and supporting opinions
- I believe / do not believe that... (because) ...
- Personally I feel that...
- Let me explain why.
- In my opinion, ...
- Just consider...
- As I see it, …
- The reason is...
- It seems to me that…
- This is because...
- I would argue that for the following reasons…
- I feel very strongly that...
- I am convinced that...
- I am of the opinion that...
- I am very much in favour of / against...
- I am completely opposed to...
- The reasons why I believe that... are as follows.

Opening phrases
- People (sometimes) claim that… but I feel that...
- It is often said / argued that... However, it seems to me that...
- It is a fact that...
- Over the past few months / years, it seems that…
- Recently, we have all become concerned that…
- Nowadays, we are all realising that...
- In the past, people used to…, but now...
- These days, it seems that…

Making statements
- It is clear that...
- On the whole, it appears / seems that...
- We must take into account the fact that...
- It goes without saying that...
- It is important to remember that...

Explaining / Expanding ideas and giving examples
- This means that...
- This is largely due to...
- For example / For instance, ...
- In other words, ...
- Take, for example, the situation in...

Listing arguments
- Firstly / In the first place / To begin with, ...
- Secondly / A second area to consider is…
- Another point to remember is...
- Finally, ...
- In conclusion, ...
- Last but not least, ...

Evaluating ideas, dismissing contrary arguments
- I think it is true that...
- I totally disagree / agree with the point that…
- It is questionable whether…
- I am sure / I doubt whether…
- It is true that... On the other hand, ...
- While nobody can deny that... , I would like to point out that…
- I agree that… However, ...
- Although it is true that, we must remember that...
- It could be argued that… However, I would like to point out that...
- Despite all the arguments, I still feel that...
- Notwithstanding the claim that... , I would argue that…
- It may be true that... , but all too often...
- In no way can I agree that...
- **Surely it is completely unacceptable that...**

Persuading
- I would urge you to consider…
- I am sure you will agree that…
- Surely you must agree that…
- I would urge you very strongly to...
- When you hear the arguments, I am sure you will agree that...

Evaluating
- I was extremely impressed by…
- I was rather disappointed by…
- The problem could easily be solved if...
- I would like to praise the...
- Another area for complaint is…
- My overall impression was that…
- I am sure that visitors / readers / holidaymakers will thoroughly enjoy...
- While some people will love... , others may feel less happy.
- A major problem is that...
- I was less happy with..

Making recommendations
- I recommend that we...
- I propose that we...
- We should also...
- I believe that we should...
- We could...
- If we were to... , we could...
- I suggest we... We would then be able to...

Summarising
- All in all, I think that...
- To sum up, I believe that...
- In conclusion, the facts suggest that...

Speaking

Giving personal information
- I'm speaking English for my own satisfaction / my job / in order to improve my employment prospects.
- I always loved (the sea).
- I'd love to visit places untouched by man.
- However, there's no place like home.
- That's a big question!
- I'm keen on...
- I haven't given it much thought until now.

Describing pictures
- What strikes me about the first picture is the fact that...
- This picture reminds me of...
- Judging from the photograph, the children...
- The man appears to be...
- From what we can see here, he must...
- There are many similarities...
- Both pictures depict...
- Both pictures are quite similar in that they show...
- When you give it a closer look it reveals...
- The first picture... whereas the other picture...
- Another important difference is...
- Picture... doesn't show... as clearly as...
- Picture... attempts to... but I think picture... does this more effectively...
- All the pictures are interesting, but... gives a stronger idea of...
- It's difficult to tell from a photograph but this picture could have been taken in...
- I might be wrong, but I'd say that this picture...
- I would imagine / guess that this picture comes from...
- Picture... is by far the best to show because...
- To me, picture... is essential for this kind of publication.
- I'm surprised there is no picture showing...
- A picture of... would get the message across more effectively.
- The name for this escapes me at present, but it's for / it's like...

Sustaining an interaction
- It's my belief...
- For my part...
- As I see it...

Describing characters / personalities
- He tends to be...
- She can be...
- He is inclined to be...
- She appears / seems to be...

Hobbies and interests
- He is crazy about... -ing.
- She loves... -ing.
- His greatest love is...
- What she loves most in life is...
- He spends all his time... -ing.

- As I was saying...
- I forgot to mention...
- I'm of the opinion that...
- To my mind...
- To my way of thinking...
- I am convinced that...
- I am inclined to believe that...
- Don't get me wrong but shouldn't we... ?
- Judging by... they must be...
- ... is a separate issue.
- Moving on to...
- I couldn't agree more.
- I agree up to a point.
- I think I see what you mean, but...
- I'm in two minds about it. / I'm ambivalent about...
- That's true in a way, I suppose, but...
- I don't feel convinced...
- That's one way of looking at it. On the other hand...
- It brings us to the question / idea / problem of ...
- Perhaps we should put... first? What do you think?
- A strong point in favour of... is that...
- What do you think should go next?
- Are you happy with this order then?
- Do you go along with that?

Expressing and justifying opinions, agreeing and / or disagreeing
- Yes, I completely agree.
- Yes, that's what I think too.
- Do you really think so?
- That's an interesting idea, but...
- I'm not sure about that.
- Just following from what X was saying, I also feel...
- While generally agreeing with X, I must say that...
- Adding to what X has just said, I think...
- I can sympathise with what X said but...
- One thing X didn't mention is...
- Perhaps it should be also emphasised that ... / it should be pointed out that...

phrasal verb	meaning	example
break down	stop working or functioning	*The telephone system broke down during the storm.*
break in / into	enter a building by force	*A gang of robbers broke into the golf club.*
break out	a) start suddenly b) escape	*A fire broke out while we were having lunch.* *The prisoner broke out of prison two days ago.*
break up	bring a relationship to an end	*They broke up in 1999 and then she married Luke.*
bring back	make somebody remember something	*That song brought back a very painful day.*
bring out	produce or publish something	*The writer brought out his second novel.*
bring up	care for and educate a child	*Caroline brought up four children by herself.*
call off	cancel	*The match was called off because of heavy rain.*
carry on	continue	*Even though he was tired, he carried on studying.*
come across	meet somebody by chance	*I came across him while I was touring the USA.*
come round / around	visit somebody for a short time	*You really must come round and see us next year.*
come up with	find a solution or have a brilliant idea	*She came up with a great idea for the new ad.*
do without	succeed in living without something	*I can't understand how they can do without TV!*
drop out	quit school or a course	*She dropped out of university after only a year.*
fall out	quarrel with somebody	*Lisa and Dave have fallen out again!*
fill in	complete a form by writing information	*To make an order fill in this form.*
get off	a) leave a train, bus, plane b) start a journey	*Can you tell me where I have to get off?* *I think it's better to get off early in the morning.*
get on / along with	like each other and have a good relation	*She gets on very well with her sister.*
get over	overcome a problem and start feeling well	*I'm sure she will get over the shock she had.*
get through to	contact somebody by telephone	*I tried many times, but I couldn't get through to him.*
give in	admit you have been defeated	*The police forced the rebels to give in.*
give out	distribute	*Why are you giving out these leaflets?*
give up	stop doing or having something	*You should give up working and relax a bit more.*
go off	a) explode b) become bad (about food)	*The bomb went off in the market square.* *What a terrible smell! The milk must have gone off.*
go on	continue	*I don't want to go on talking about the same things!*
go out	stop burning	*Suddenly the lights went out.*
go out with	have a romantic relationship	*Cindy is going out with an Italian boy.*
go over	revise or examine carefully	*Go over the test before you hand it in.*
hold on	wait to talk to somebody (on the phone)	*Can you hold on? Let me see if Tim is here.*
keep away	avoid going near somebody or something	*Keep away from the pier! It's dangerous.*
keep in	restrain	*Don't keep your anger in!*
keep on	continue	*The snow kept on falling for three days.*
keep up with	learn about the latest news or events	*She always keeps up with the latest fashion trends.*

Phrasal Verbs

phrasal verb	meaning	example
live through	survive after an unpleasant situation	Mr Sword has lived through the Second World War.
look after	take care of	Laurie, can you look after my daughter tomorrow?
look forward to	wait for something pleasant	I'm looking forward to seeing her again.
look into	examine deeply and carefully	A special committee will look into the matter.
look out	be careful	Look out! A bee is flying around you.
look up	look for information in a reference book	I had to look these words up in the dictionary.
make into	change into something or somebody else	This poem was made into a song after many years.
make off	hurry away to escape	The pickpockets made off on foot.
make out	manage to see or hear clearly	She could make out a person in the darkness.
make up	invent a story	I often make up funny stories for my niece.
make up with	become friendly again after an argument	Don't worry, he'll make up with her by tonight.
pick up	go and collect someone in a car	I'll pick you up at 8 p.m., OK?
put off	postpone	The match will be put off if it rains.
put on	a) gain (usually weight) b) wear clothes	I think he has put on about three kilos. It's very cold. Why don't you put your coat on?
put out	stop something from burning	Excuse me, can you put your cigarette out, please?
put through	connect by telephone	Could you put me through to the headmaster, please?
put up	let somebody stay at your home	I'm sorry, but I can't put you up for the night.
run across / into	meet somebody by chance	I've just run across Dave! He's here for a few days.
run out of	finish a supply of something	The car stopped because it had run out of fuel.
run over	a) knock somebody down (with a vehicle) b) read something quickly	An old lady was run over by a truck yesterday. You had better run over your notes again.
set off	begin a journey	What time are you going to set off for Madrid?
talk over	discuss a problem	You should talk your problem over with an expert.
take after	look like a member of your family	Your niece really takes after you.
take down	write something down	The secretary quickly took the message down.
take off	leave the ground and fly (plane)	The plane couldn't take off due to thick fog.
take up	start doing something regularly	He decided to take up playing the guitar.
throw out / away	get rid of something you no longer need	Why don't you throw out / away that old sweater?
try on	put on clothes to see how they fit	Try these trousers on before buying them.
turn down	refuse an offer or a proposal	I think he'll turn your invitation down.
turn down / up	reduce / increase (volume or heating)	Can you turn the volume of the radio down / up?
turn on / off	start / stop a machine (pressing a button)	He didn't want to turn the TV on / off.
turn out	a) happen in a particular way b) prove to be	The party turned out very well. The book turned out to be really exciting.
turn up	arrive	Your friends haven't turned up yet.
work out	find a solution or an answer	The President is trying to work out a compromise.

Test 1

Track 1 Part 1, p. 24

1

Mark Hi, Irene. I haven't seen you for ages. Have you been hiding yourself away?

Irene I must admit I haven't been very sociable for the last couple of months. Busy, busy! What about you?

Mark Nothing special. I'm still working at the call centre giving people advice on how to use their mobile phones. I bet you're doing something much more exciting.

Irene It depends on what you mean by that! I've got a job designing the covers for a series of fantasy books.

Mark Fantasy books? Does that mean you get to draw pictures of weird supernatural characters?

Irene Exactly. The stories are mainly about fights between the good and evil! I have to show that on the covers.

Mark You must have to use a lot of imagination. It's very different from my job where I just give out facts.

Irene One fact that I know is that you earn a lot more money than I do!

Mark True. It's some compensation for having to do the same thing every day.

2

Mrs Jones Good morning. I have an appointment to see the Head. My name is Lisa Jones.

Assistant Good morning, Mrs Jones. Umm – according to her diary, you arranged to meet her at ten thirty.

Mrs Jones I know I'm a bit early, but I was hoping to see her as soon as possible. My daughter's a student here.

Assistant It's only just gone ten, so I'm afraid you'll have to wait for a while. Can I get you a cup of tea?

Mrs Jones No, thank you. I'm very anxious to speak to her. It won't take very long. If she's in her office, could I go in and have a word?

Assistant I'm afraid she's teaching at the moment. Her lesson ends at ten fifteen and then she usually pops into the staffroom to see the teachers. I'll let you know as soon as she's back in her office.

Mrs Jones I didn't realise that headteachers had to spend time in the classroom as well as doing all their other duties.

3

Kevin You're through to Horizon Television. My name's Kevin. How can I help you?

Rebecca Hello, Kevin. I'm Rebecca Sharp. I'm waiting for an engineer to come and install my 4G television, but he hasn't arrived yet.

Kevin I'm very sorry to hear that, madam. Can you give me your account number?

Rebecca My account number? Where can I find it?

Kevin It should be on the letter we sent you. It has nine digits starting with eight seven eight.

Rebecca I can't remember seeing it. Can't you just type in my name to get into my account?

Kevin Unfortunately, our company insists we only use the number to access customers' accounts for security reasons.

Rebecca I suppose I'll have to go and look for it and then make another call. It's very inconvenient.

Kevin I apologise but I have to follow the rules.

4

This summer we're launching our latest cruise ship which is going to have a different focus. People often think that going on a cruise is for people who just want to sit by the pool or visit ancient monuments. Not on this one! We've designed it especially to look after the needs of young people. We have a wide range of activities to keep them happy. These include a sports club where they can learn diving, judo and karate – the sorts of activities they might not have tried before. There are trained instructors and we provide all the equipment. We also know young people have a lot of energy and need a range of activities to keep them busy. We have a programme of competitions in art, music and dance. The winners will be decided by a panel of celebrity judges who will be joining us on board. I'm sorry I can't tell you who they are at the moment, but I can guarantee that our young cruisers will be very happy to meet them!

5

Customer Good morning. I want to send this package first class, please.

Worker Yes, of course. I just have to ask you first of all – what's inside the packet?

Customer Why on earth do you need to do that?

Worker Well, sir. There are certain items that are prohibited and I'm required to check before I can proceed.

Customer I'm not happy at all about having to tell you, but if I have to – it's a birthday present for my mother.

Worker Very nice, sir – but what exactly is the present?

Customer It's just a present, don't you understand? It's a very special day for her and I can't be with her, so I want to get her something she'll like.

Worker I appreciate that but unfortunately, I still need to know what the present is.

Customer Oh, very well. It's an expensive bottle of perfume.

Worker I'm sorry to tell you but sending perfume is not allowed.

Customer If you won't do it, I'll just have to go somewhere else.

6

Tom Have you met our new neighbour yet?

Susan Yes, I went round yesterday to introduce myself. What about you?

Tom I saw her going into her house and waved but I haven't spoken to her. What's she like?

Susan She seems very nice but a bit shy. I suggested that I got all our friends together at my house so she could meet them, but she said she'd rather wait and get to know them individually. She told me that she used to live in a small village where nothing much happened and she had to drive to go shopping or to have a meal.

Tom We're so lucky here to have everything we need on our doorstep. However, if she's still got a car, she's going to have difficulty parking it.

Susan Don't worry. She did exactly the same as I did and sold her car. I think she realised that the public transport around here is so good you don't need to have one.

Tom Very sensible. Now, as I haven't had the chance to talk to her, why don't we go round now and invite her out for a coffee.

Susan Good idea. We can find out a bit more about her. I'm sure she'll start to relax when she sees we want her to become part of our community.

7

First up is a musical. You can't go wrong if you choose the London Palladium. It's right next to Oxford Circus underground station. There's an all-star cast in a new production of Cats based on the poems written by TS Elliot.
How about a modern play? The best place to see recently written drama is at the Royal Court Theatre in Sloane Square in the very fashionable district of Chelsea. You may have heard of it because of the famous football club. Their latest offering is *The Woods* by Alan Evans. We now move on to plays that are called 'revivals'. This means that they've been staged many times before but continue to be popular. We think the best revival on offer this month is a delightful production of an old favourite: *The Rivals* by R.B. Sheridan.
It was first seen where it's on now – the Covent Garden – as long ago as January 1775.
Finally, a visit to London wouldn't be complete without seeing a play by William Shakespeare. There are many excellent productions of his works including *Hamlet* at the National Theatre. However, we strongly believe that a work by the Bard is best seen at the Globe Theatre on the south bank of the River Thames.

8

Assistant Good morning. How can I help?

Customer Morning. I'm not sure under the circumstances that it is 'good'. However, I hope it will get better during our conversation.

Assistant You obviously have a problem with something. Please could you explain what it is?

Customer Well. My girlfriend likes to burn candles in the evening. She particularly enjoys the ambience they create. However, she bought one from this shop last week. It's inside glass, I suppose, to make sure the flame doesn't go out.

Transcripts

Assistant I know the type you mean. There's a cylinder of glass surrounding the candle which sits on a stone base. They're very popular.

Customer They may be popular, but they are also extremely dangerous. Last night, the candle had been burning for only a couple of minutes, when the glass shattered into tiny pieces. One of them could easily have gone into my eye. I was shocked.

Assistant I'm extremely sorry, sir. Have you, by any chance, brought the candle with you, so I can have a look at it?

Customer Of course not. You don't expect me to wander into town carrying a bag full of broken glass, do you?

Assistant I'm sure you'll understand that without seeing the damage to the product, I can't give you a refund.

Track 2   Part 2, p. 25

Elliot

Thank you for inviting me to talk on the subject of extra-terrestrial activity. I have to admit that I find it absolutely fascinating and I hope you can share my interest. First of all, I want to give you a definition of what it is. I'll then leave it up to you to decide how to interpret it. The words 'extra-terrestrial' have their origins in the Latin language and mean: 'outside of the limits of the Earth'. Extra-terrestrial activity has been reported in many different parts of the world, from Warminster, a small town in southern England, to an area south of the Peruvian capital, Lima, where there appear to be runways for alien spacecraft! I want to focus on one particular incident and leave it up to you to decide whether it is fact or fiction! On the seventh of July nineteen forty-seven in the town of Roswell, which is in New Mexico in the south-west of the United States, a farm worker called William Brazel discovered some unusual materials in a field. He took them to the local police station and the Sheriff was so concerned he immediately reported the discovery to officers at the nearby base of the US air force.

The next day, a local newspaper printed a story that a 'flying disk' had crashed. However, later in the day, scientists visited the area and the story seemed to change. At a press conference, a government official stated that the 'flying disk' was actually a weather balloon. Although this story was initially accepted, there were later reports that there was no balloon anywhere near Roswell on that day. For the next thirty-one years, the story was largely forgotten until the National Enquirer, a newspaper which often prints stories about conspiracies, suggested that the government had not fully explained what had happened because they wanted to cover up or hide the discovery of alien spacecraft.

Reporters interviewed several people who claimed to have seen these strange materials scattered over a wide area. One person stated he'd seen an unusual object on fire shortly before it crashed.

The most shocking story came from a nurse who had accidentally walked into a hospital room where doctors were examining three strange creatures who looked almost human but with small bodies, thin arms and enormous heads. In nineteen ninety-seven, the National Security Agency finally published a full report into the incident. It concluded that the so-called alien bodies were in fact test dummies that are used to simulate what happens to people in a plane crash. These findings still did not persuade a lot of people that something very unusual had taken place. Roswell is now an important centre for people who believe that creatures from other planets have visited Earth. On the anniversary of the publication of the story, thousands of people attend a festival which highlights the paranormal.

There are seminars, workshops and visits to the site where it was believed the flying object landed. Despite all the excitement about this incident, I'm afraid that there's still no definite evidence to show that the town has had extraterrestrial visitors! However, I'm still unsure about what really happened. To finish my talk, I want to put both sides of the argument and then, as I said at the beginning, give you an opportunity to make up your own minds. There's no doubt that something curious happened in the town of Roswell all those years ago. However, scientists have been unable to find any objects that have not originated from earth and no photographs of unidentified flying objects were taken. On the other hand, there are many people who are convinced that aliens came to earth at Roswell, but the United States government is so worried about the consequences that they continue to hide the truth from the general public. Before you reach your own conclusions, I'm happy to answer any questions.

Track 3   Part 3, p. 26

Speaker 1

We really enjoyed our evening when we all went to see the play, apart from a slightly strange experience we had before we went in. There's a tapas restaurant right next to the theatre that we had been to before. We had had lunch there a couple of weeks before. It's only just opened, so we thought it wouldn't be particularly busy. As soon as we went in, a member of staff asked us if we'd booked. We told him we hadn't and even though there were empty tables, he then said we had to wait for an hour before he could find seats for us. That really annoyed me as we only had an hour and a half before the play started. Anyway, we found a nice Italian place that was opposite. The meal was delicious and it was very good value for money.

Speaker 2

The play is very well written with lots of twists and turns, so you are never quite sure what is going to happen next. I really liked that, but during the interval we went to have coffee and we overheard some people sitting next to us in the theatre café. They were complaining that they had absolutely no idea what was going on and they couldn't understand some of the actors because they were speaking very quickly. In the second half, the mystery was cleverly resolved and it had a happy ending. On the way out of the theatre, the same couple were still going on about how awful it was and they had wasted their evening. However, we had a great time.

Speaker 3

The theatre where we saw the play is over a hundred years old and the seats are not that comfortable because there isn't much leg room. However, the way the play was staged is very modern and was done in a very clever way. The action was in many different places: a hotel lobby, a train station, a train compartment and a sitting room in a house. They managed to change the scenery very quickly, so that the audience hardly noticed what was happening. The sets were very realistic and very well constructed. I found it really satisfying to watch it because the acting was good, the characters in the play were interesting but most of all because of the brilliant way it was presented.

Speaker 4

One of the actors in the play is very famous, mainly for the work she's done on TV. We were sitting in the front row and it was fantastic to see her close up. I like to sit there because there's no one in front of you and I can also stretch my legs. You obviously have to pay a bit more to sit there than in other parts of the theatre, but I think it's well worth it. At the end of the play when all the cast come and bow to the audience, you're near enough to be able to shake their hands! If you sit a long way back, you don't get nearly such a good view.

Speaker 5

I thought the play was really entertaining because of the way it was performed. The man and woman who had the lead roles had to show a whole range of emotions, from fear and despair to anger and at the end, joy and happiness. There were also some scenes where there were fights. They were done really well, especially as they involved several people. One of the best scenes was when they were on the train and they were trying to escape from some bad people who were after them. Even though they were just pretending to shoot at them, it looked very realistic and you could imagine that it was moving along the rails.

Track 4   Part 4, p. 27

Tom Sometimes the news can be a bit depressing, but one story really cheered me up.

Helen What's that, Tom?

Tom Landing a space vehicle on the surface of Mars. What a scientific achievement!

Helen I don't know very much about it. Are you sure you didn't read about it in one of those science fiction graphic novels you like buying?

Tom I must admit it sounds closer to science fiction than science fact – but it really did happen.

Helen Give me some more information about it and then I'll decide whether you're telling the truth.

Tom OK – this is the story of the event. NASA – that's the North American Space Agency – launched a spacecraft called InSight that took six months to travel the three hundred million miles from Earth to the red planet – that's Mars, of course.

Helen That's a very long way. It must have been travelling at a very high speed through space to get there.

Tom It certainly was. Its speed was around twenty-eight thousand kilometres per hour and then in the seven minutes or so before it landed, its speed had to drop down to about the same as a person jogging – not even running or sprinting – just jogging.

Helen That sounds incredible. I wonder how they managed to enable it to slow down to that degree.

Tom I don't know enough about science to even begin to understand. All I know is that it landed safely in the northern hemisphere and started sending back pictures almost immediately. There was another rocket called Beagle that landed, but then mysteriously disappeared. It was such a relief.

Helen What was the aim of this Mars mission?

Tom The scientists are interested in the core of Mars – that's the inside of the planet. They want to know whether it's solid or liquid. One person described it very well as the difference between an uncooked egg and a hard-boiled egg.

Helen I've never thought of Mars being like an egg. Are there other experiments?

Tom There certainly are. They want to listen for marsquakes. They're like earthquakes, but they happen on Mars. Scientists listen for vibrations which give information about the types of rock Mars is made of.

Helen It all sounds fascinating, but why do we actually need to know about Mars? Surely there are enough problems on Earth without having to worry about what's going on in outer space. There's little likelihood that people are going to live there, especially as I'm sure there isn't any water.

Tom According to a report I read from one of InSight's chief scientists, studying what's under the surface of Mars helps us to understand how the planets in the solar system evolved. It enables us to understand why we can sit in the sun and get a tan on Earth, compared to Venus where you'll burn in seconds or Mars where you'll freeze to death.

Helen I know where I'd rather be. I now accept that this actually took place, but it still reminds me of the comics I used to read.

Tom Have a look at the online video showing what happened at NASA headquarters when InSight landed successfully. The people who had spent years planning it went crazy with excitement and everyone started clapping and hugging each other. Even though it had taken a long time, you could see how much they believed in each other. The other important factor is that a lot of other countries are helping with this Mars mission. For example, there's something called TWINS which stands for Temperature and Winds for InSight which monitors the weather at the landing site. That was constructed by the Spanish Astrobiology Center. The Italian Space Agency also contributed by providing highly sophisticated laser equipment. These are hugely important steps in creating greater understanding between scientists. It's not like in the old days where there was so much rivalry and countries competed against each other in what was known as the 'Space Race'.

Test 2

Track 5   Part 1, p. 46

1

It was one of those 'must-see' moments. Everybody I knew watched it, and everybody at work the next day was talking about it. It was just like that soap opera years ago when the guy got shot and all you could hear the next day was people discussing who shot him. There were even T-shirts printed 'Who shot BJ?' they said. Or like that world cup final where the England player used his hand to score a goal and the referee said the goal was valid. I'm sure there must be something to explain how she did it though, you can't just make Buckingham Palace disappear into thin air. But it was really dramatic to say the least.

2

I just don't see the point of them. You get on the tube and some adolescent sits next to you and all you hear is this tinny repetitive beat. Why can't they just put headphones on? Why do they imagine that the rest of us want to hear their music? It's not as if I've ever heard anybody using them to play decent music. I used to think their ringtones were annoying, but it's nothing compared to these. It really ruins my journey to work sometimes. Not that it was ever really a pleasure.

3

I know exactly how you must feel. But just let me explain… I know, I know… I got the two thirty train and I was supposed to get the connecting train at two fifteen, but there was a delay at the train station and we didn't get there until half past two and I'd missed it. The next one wasn't until 5. Can you believe it? I've a good mind to write a letter of complaint to the company and tell them how angry I am; it's not as if the tickets are cheap either. You know how much I wanted to meet you, how can I make it up to you? What? Yes, I know… of course I had it with me… just that I forgot to charge it last night and it ran out of batteries, so I couldn't call you. Hello? Hello?

4

It's because I have these allergies. I've tried everything. Creams, pills… you name it. The doctor told me he wasn't sure what was causing it, he even suggested it was all in my head. But surely I'm not imagining the rashes I get when I eat them. It just started a couple of years ago, I used to eat plenty of them with no problem. I suppose it must be something to do with the fertilizers and pesticides they use these days. So, no, those look nice and I'm sure they're fine but I don't want to risk it, I'll have the organic ones instead. A kilo should be enough.

5

Seriously, there are times when I think I just can't take any more. I love her to bits of course, but at times, well, you can imagine, I just have to take a deep breath and count to 20 or I'll just explode or end up walking out. She's always been the same, ever since we were little kids. You just can't get a word in edgeways. She'd kill me if she knew, but sometimes when she calls I just put the phone on the table, go away and make a cup of coffee and when I come back she's still going on and on and none the wiser.

6

F John! I haven't seen you for ages. How are you?

M Sara! Hi! You look great. I suppose you must still be taking those classes.

F I sure am! I've lost 5 kilos since I last saw you. Anna's a real dictator in her classes; she really makes you work and sweat. But I have plenty of time these days since I finished at university. What about you? How come I haven't seen you there for so long?

M Well, time is the big problem really. I've got so much work to do, I ended up finishing so late and then taking work home with me. There just don't seem to be enough hours in the day. But I do seem to be putting on a bit of weight, so maybe I'll try to get down there at least once next week.

7

I know I said I'd be home by 8 but it just can't be done. I've got a huge stack of work on my desk and I promised my boss I'd have it done by Wednesday. I'm going to have to come in early before he gets here at eight thirty tomorrow and get some more of it done. Look, it's half past eight now, I'll just put in another hour and then I'll finish, OK? Do we need anything from the shops on my way home?

8

It's quite breathtaking really. You could almost be there. It's such a beautiful park, the valley looks gorgeous. You can see why it attracts so many visitors. Only last week John was asking me if I fancied going camping with him there for a long weekend. But that's why they made it really, to highlight how so many visitors going there every year is eroding a lot of the natural vegetation that the wildlife there rely on for food and shelter. Really did make me think. And the music they used is great, really complimented the images. You should see it.

Track 6   Part 2, p. 47

Checking in at Blackpool airport couldn't be easier. The majority of check-in desks at Blackpool Airport are located on the first floor of the terminal building. Air UK operates its UK, London and German flights from check-in Area 14, which is located on a level beneath the Arrivals Hall.

To save time, have your tickets and passport ready, and ensure your hand luggage contains only the items you may need during your journey. Ensure that carry-on luggage does not contain any liquids, gels or pastes that exceed 100 ml. You can also use the self-service check-in desks. Self-service check-in is available to passengers departing from the Airport travelling with certain airlines. A number of scheduled airlines offer self service check-in and Internet check-in technologies in order to facilitate their passengers with early check-in, seat selection and issue of boarding passes. Please select from the airline links below to see if this service applies to your destination. Airline staff are on hand should you require any assistance. Sit back and relax in the Eric Morecambe Departure lounge. Enjoy the comfort and relaxing atmosphere of the Eric Morecambe Lounge for up to three hours – for only €25 per person. We offer an excellent service to all passengers regardless of airline or class of ticket. And there's a 20% discount for the over 60s who can take advantage of our facilities for only 20 euros per person. Facilities include: complementary refreshments; newspapers and magazines; free Wi-Fi access throughout the lounge and notification of delays and flight times. A left luggage facility is available in the Car Park Atrium, directly across the road from the Terminal, for short and long term storage of luggage. The facility is open from 6 a.m. to 11 p.m. daily and rates vary depending on the size of baggage. A car key holding facility exists for passengers, at a charge, with Greencaps, in the Car Park Atrium. The keys must be collected by the person nominated to do so. This person must have photographic identification when collecting the keys. Those leaving keys must also provide a reference of where their car is parked. Blackpool airport boasts a variety of cafés and restaurants, such as the Cosy Café located on the mezzanine floor. Relax in this modern light filled restaurant and choose from a wonderful selection of modern Irish classics such as Pan fried Chicken with creamy smoked bacon and Leek sauce, freshly cooked pasta dishes, or Pan Asian delights such as Thaistyle prawns. Full English breakfast is served from 4 a.m. The airport isconveniently located approximately 10 km north of Blackpool city centre. It is served by a large number of buses, coaches and taxis all allowing you to get to and from the airport with ease. Over 21 million passengers travelled through Blackpool Airport last year.

Track 7   Part 3, p. 48

Speaker 1

I thought I'd be a lot more anxious than I was. I couldn't sleep for a few days before it. I kept going over the worst possible scenarios in my head. Everything from forgetting my lines, to throwing up all over the stage… I even imagined a fire in the theatre. I suppose it's only natural really. I mean it's your very first time in front of an audience, how are you expected to feel? There were hundreds of people there! But at the end of the day, you've done your preparation. You've spent months with the play, living the part… so when I stepped out on the stage I was surprised at myself. I didn't even notice the audience; I just went out and played my part as though it was the most natural thing in the world. And that's how it felt, it wasn't me up there on stage, I was the character and every line was my own.

Speaker 2

I couldn't wait to get out there. Seriously. We'd rehearsed it so often I was eager to show people what we'd done, what a classic play it was. The play was set during the First World War and was about a group of soldiers all from the same village. who all get killed on the same day. We'd read so many letters, plays and books from the men who were actually there and what we noticed in the early days of the war was how so many men were so keen to go out and fight, even if it meant certain death. At the time I remember thinking they were crazy… but it's strange, the more we practiced on our own in an empty theatre… the more we just wanted to go out and do the real thing in front of a real audience… even if it proved to be a total disaster. Which it wasn't, I'm pleased to say. We got very good reviews in the following week's local paper.

Speaker 3

It was maybe the most frightening moment of my life. I was waiting in the wings, I knew my cue was coming up any minute. My mind went blank. I started hyperventilating. My stomach was in knots. I started to sweat. I nearly ran away there and then. I just wanted to hide and wished I'd never put myself in this position. I couldn't though, I couldn't let all those people down. The people who'd bought tickets but more importantly all my fellow actors and the director… we'd all worked so very hard to make this production. So I took a few deep breaths

and when the time came I went onto the stage. I'd like to say I delivered a breathtaking performance but the truth is I was terrible. It did get better after that first performance though, thankfully.

Speaker 4

I wasn't supposed to be appearing that day. I was the understudy to Jake Collins, the Hollywood film star. He was in London to perform in this play and the publicity it got was astonishing, you couldn't turn on the television or open a newspaper without seeing his picture or an article about the play. So a lot of excitement had been created in the city. I imagine a lot of the audience had bought tickets simply to see a Hollywood star up close. They must have been rather disappointed when it was announced that he wouldn't be performing due to food poisoning. But for me it was a wonderful opportunity, and you can't imagine how great standing in for such a famous actor made me feel. Especially as when the play finished nobody I saw leaving the theatre looked in the least bit disappointed.

Speaker 5

It was a nightmare from the beginning to the end. I couldn't focus, I had trouble remembering my lines, I could barely move. Honestly, I was shattered. I had given up my job as a teacher just 9 months before to pursue my dream of being a professional actor, and as luck would have it my wife announced that she was pregnant just a week later. I'll have to make a decent job of this I thought, I've now got more responsibility than I've ever had. We were both so happy when I got this part, it was quite a prestigious production and it looked like I might have a future. Of course, fate had other ideas. My wife went into the hospital the day before the first performance. I was up for 30 hours straight that day, pacing up and down the corridors. She gave birth to our daughter, Chloe, just 2 hours before curtains up. I literally had to run all the way from the hospital to the theatre. Luckily everybody understood and I actually received an award for that role.

Track 8   Part 4, p. 49

F Steven Pride is a difficult man to track down. The co-founder and GEO of MusicFlow is busy travelling around Europe on business. Founded in 2008, MusicFlow is quickly gaining a legion of loyal fans and it is easy to understand why. The musicstreaming program gives users instant access to a huge catalogue of music from all over the world, free of charge.
Unlike the majority of similar websites, MusicFlow's beauty lies in the fact that it works with music companies and rights holders so that its operations are wholly legitimate. This explains why MusicFlow has been welcomed with open arms by both producers and consumers of music alike. Just this past Wednesday saw Steven Pride attending the Brit Awards in London, mingling with the crème de la crème of the music industry. This would never have been the case for the likes of Phapster or Pirate Ship.
So it was with great satisfaction that Steven Pride, very much the man of the moment, took some time out to answer our questions.;
You are often described as a hardnosed businessman, are there any other things you are also guilty of?

M Right now, with all the travelling I'm doing, I'm not getting enough sleep at night, so I'd have to say falling asleep in meetings. My wife might tell you I work too hard, but I don't think that's true. I'm just doing what I love.

F Who has most inspired you?

M In terms of music I would have to say The Beatles. I don't think we'll ever see any group produce such a body of work ever again. Almost every song is a classic. In terms of business, I think my father has been my biggest influence, he always told me I should just do what makes me happy. And for everything else, my wife. She's been my rock, my inspiration, an oasis of stability over the last few years, which have been crazy.

F Go on, give us a quick look into your music collection. Who are you listening to right now?

M There are some fantastic artists coming through, such as We are Scientists, Vampire Weekend, Bats for Lashes, Fleet Foxes and The Black Keys. Leonard Cohen's latest is awesome and I've just started listening to Little Feat's new album, which just hit MusicFlow today.

F MusicFlow was yours and Marta Pirez's brainchild, did it come about quickly from a chat you both had or was the idea a long process development?

M It's something we'd been thinking about for a while. One thing that became obvious to us about person-to-person file sharing was the fact that people consumed more music than ever from a bigger diversity of artists. The influences in terms of what they were listening to were coming more from friends than from radio stations. They were consuming music like crazy but weren't necessarily paying for that music.

The underlying demand for music was bigger than ever.

The reason we set up MusicFlow was to cater for that demand but to also, at the same time, create a functioning revenue stream.

F What has been MusicFlow's biggest challenge since start-up?

M Well obviously signing the various record deals was a huge step for us. We want to be the alternative to music piracy and to have the support of the record labels, both the majors and independents, to allow us to realise that aim. Since then, probably dealing with the surge in users has been one of our biggest challenges, as well as adding on average 10,000 tracks a day to the MusicFlow catalogue. Putting all the world's music in one place is a big job.

F Who do you see as your biggest competition?

M Depending on who you speak to, we will be compared to different services. In the UK, we get compared to First.fm; in France a lot of people compare us to Geezer, while in the US a lot of people see us as similar to Phapster. I honestly believe that we don't have a main competitor on that level as no one is currently offering what we are offering in terms of an ad-supported model and a subscription model as one.

F What have you got planned for next year?

M Lots of stuff. We've got some unbelievably cool exclusive content available for our users coming up over the next few months, plus we're also going to provide our MusicFlow Premium subscribers with some special extra services.

Test 3

Track 9   Part 1, p. 68

1

Well, I've got to say, much as I liked taking part, it got a bit too much in the end. What with training twice a week and then the match on Sunday... and I'm not getting any younger. I found I needed Monday and Tuesday just to recover from all the aches and pains. And I've got so much on my plate at the moment... I've found that since I stopped it has really freed up my week and I can see a lot more of the family than I did.

2

I just browsed their catalogue on their website, made a note of the model number and drove into their out-of-town place to pay for it and pick it up. I must say they're certainly doing good business... queues like you wouldn't believe. You can see why the local furniture market is suffering; the whole town must have been in there buying things for the house or garden.

3

About time too, we've been crying out for this for years. Kids have had to travel into Nottcaster. It took my nephew close to an hour to get in there by bus and after his various sports teams he wasn't getting home until nearly nine o'clock. Finally it looks like they're doing something for this community instead of spending money on things there's no real need for. I mean, that procession last year… what was that for? A waste of money if you ask me.

4

Well, there have been rumours flying around for months. You just hope that it's not going to be you. I know it sounds selfish but our department is one of the most productive in the whole company; we don't get a moment's peace. But... it turns out that the whole company is suffering and there'll be large scale redundancies. Hopefully if they let me go I can find something similar; I'm too old now to retrain and do something completely different.

5

How would you like to sleep on the banks of majestic Lake Victoria, listening to the gentle lapping of the lake on the shore, and the wildlife of the nearby National Reserve Park? Just what you need after an actionpacked day of canoeing, rock climbing or scuba diving. Lake Victoria Hotel offers 2 weeks in its luxury compound, where you can do as much or as little as your heart desires. See our website for further details.

6

It's a joke really, they were putting so many questions to him and he didn't have a clue. I really don't think he stands a chance of winning the next election if he carries on like this. I had to laugh when they asked him about his foreign policy... his answer just seemed to make no sense at all. He came over as a bit of a clown.

7

Well, I thought that at that price you can't go wrong. But I started to regret it once I saw the size of the box, it only just fit into the car. The thing with these flat pack things... there's just so many bits and pieces. When I got home and started looking at the instructions... well... I didn't know which was up and which was down. Finally I got it all together and it fits quite well next to the sofa. Hopefully it will stay upright for a while, although I can't be certain it will.

8

Well, when I saw the adverts for tickets, I jumped at the chance. It's years since they've played here. I suppose it's all down to their new manager, he's really got them playing well. What an atmosphere it will be... the lights, the singing, the drama of it all... I can't wait. It's great that this town can stage an event like this. And they've got a really good chance of going all the way and winning the cup this year.

Track 10   Part 2, p. 69

Brian Daniels, co-founder of The Wentworth Art Fair, has announced that a controversial collection of Phillipa West will be the subject of this year's Wentworth Art Festival Symposium. The two-day event will bring together an international panel of experts to view the Marta Costello Collection made up of approximately 1,200 drawings, journals, letters, paintings and other items whose owners maintain are made by Phillipa West. Some experts on the artist's work have questioned the authenticity of the collection. The panel will present an overview of the methods and challenges of authenticating newly revealed art works. Of particular interest, in conjunction with the Wentworth Art Fair symposium, a group of the disputed objects will be on view for the first time in the United Kingdom. The symposium will take place on Saturday, February 6 and Sunday, February 7, from 10.00 a.m. to 12.00 noon at the Cheeseman Gallery at Dame Doris Brown High School for the Performing and Visual Arts, 13 Church Street. Admission is included in the purchase of an art fair ticket. Daily tickets are 10 pounds and a three-day pass is 25 pounds. Doors will open at 9.30 a.m., seating is limited and is on a first come, first served basis. Visit www.wentworthartfestival. com for further details. Approximately 20 objects from the Marta Costello Collection, including paintings, drawings, journal pages and other items, will be exhibited, and for the first time will provide experts with the opportunity to examine the controversial material. The Wentworth Art Fair Symposium panels will bring together the owners of the Costello material, experts they have enlisted to examine the material, the publisher of a recently released book on the collection, plus scholars and art dealers who have followed the controversy since it began. The moderator will be Michael Edward Hall, art historian, critic and correspondent for Art Newspaper. Moderator and journalist Michael Edward Hall says, 'The discussion will range from the specific – a description of the Costello archive – to general questions about how newly discovered artworks are received and evaluated by the scholarly community and the market.' Welsh artist Phillipa West is among the most popular and beloved women painters of the 20th century. Her paintings, which can command large sums, describe a life full of joy and love for her husband, the painter Donald Rivers. Today she is an icon, and even scraps of paper associated with her are valued not only financially but also as relics of a legendary historical figure. Her reputation is such that the Welsh Arts Council has designated her work 'National Patrimony' and restricted its trade and export. Little wonder that the Costello collection of Phillipa West material has come under such intense scrutiny. Even before the works became widely known with the April release of the illustrated book Finding Phillipa West the collection became the focus of numerous articles in major publications in Europe. Some reports celebrated the discovery of new material related to West while others questioned the authenticity of the objects and challenged their publication. The Wentworth Art Fair Symposium will look into the issues surrounding the collection and its still unresolved status.

Track 11   Part 3, p.70

Speaker 1

It's a bit of a guilty pleasure really. It's not the sort of thing I would normally have any interest in. I just happened to be browsing through one of the tabloids when I was at the dentist's and I noticed that one of the people in it went to my old school. Not that I knew her of course, I must be at least ten years older than her. But that evening I switched it on and I've been hooked ever since. I don't think I'd ever really understood the appeal before... but the thing is, they've put ordinary people in an unreal situation and you can't help but wonder how you'd react in the same situation. It's quite compulsive, it really is.

Speaker 2

Don't get me started on that... I can't tell you the amount of arguments I've had with my flatmates about it. They have it on for hours every day. Day in day out. I think it's ludicrous. What on earth people find so fascinating about it, I'll never know. They just spend hours sitting around chattering about the most trivial things. And the people they get to go on it... I wouldn't want to have to spend half an hour sitting next to them on the bus, let alone choose to watch them on television. They just want to be famous without actually having any sort of talent. No, why it's become so popular is beyond me.

Speaker 3

These days I can't say I watch it. I used to when it first started. Then it seemed to have some sort of intellectual facade... like it was a social experiment. They'd have a psychologist analysing each of the housemates' behaviour and I found that really interesting. What's more I'd notice some of that behaviour in my everyday life and I'd be able to relate what I'd learnt... I've always been fascinated by body language and things like that. But the last few series they seem to have just forgotten about that side of things and it's just entertainment, a circus act for people desperate for their 15 minutes of fame.

Speaker 4

The first couple of series, I never missed an episode but I must say that my interest has faded a bit. I have it on every now and again but I can't say I could even tell you all the names of the contestants. Though there's one guy called Tony of course. I remember him because he looks like my boyfriend's brother and they even have the same name. He's rather embarrassed about it actually... people keep coming up to him and asking him if he's Tony... and what can he say? He is Tony. We were all at the cinema with him last week when somebody asked him for his autograph... I thought he'd just explode!

Speaker 5

I couldn't tell you a thing about it I'm afraid. I know it's tremendously popular and I'm always hearing people at work or on the train talking about the people who are on it... and the way they talk about them... you'd think they were friends or neighbours. I've got nothing against it really, and there must be something to it if so many people are addicted to it... it's just that I've been going to pilates classes three times a week and by the time I get home it's nearly over... and besides, my favourite detective show... McCallister is just about to start on the other side, so I sit down and watch that, I never miss it. It's great!

Track 12   Part 4, p. 71

M Moving away from home is a big step and one most of us make when we go off to college or university. The chances are you'll find yourself sharing a house or a flat. We've invited Dr. Victoria Millington into the studio to discuss problems with sharing accommodation and strategies for anticipating and dealing with them.

F Sharing a house or a flat can be daunting, but it can be fun, too. One of the most rewarding things about living in a shared household is the social side. There's always someone to talk to; you never have to be alone unless you wish to be. Among the best time you'll have living with others is when you share with friends. Also, it's very handy to share if you want to move out of home, but can't afford your own flat. And as long as the basic rules and routines are clear, it's much more interesting than living on your own.

M What's the most common problem people face when sharing?

F One of the most contentious areas when living in a shared household has got to be cleanliness, or lack thereof. Some people are, frankly, lazy. At the other end of

the scale, some flatmates hover over you while you're eating your dinner and when you pause at the end of your meal, they demand you wash up your plate immediately. There are several approaches to this problem and you and your flatmates will have to decide which is the best approach for you. Maybe the best and most obvious idea is to make a rota. Some people find this restrictive, but it's a fair system and if you work it out well beforehand, it can really pay off. It's up to you how you arrange it: you could make sure each person takes responsibility for one room or alternate all the jobs that need to be done. However, it is essential that everyone sticks to the plan, otherwise half of you will feel resentful and the others will feel guilty. Sometimes it can be difficult to keep up with the rota due to changing circumstances, so factor in some flexibility – think about taking turns for having a week off, for example.

M What are other common problems?

F Space is another serious matter. In order to get on well with your flatmates, communal space is important. Just think about it. Living in a flat with no meeting place other than a small kitchen, say, will mean that you'll never get friendlier than just saying hello politely and exchanging a few words. It's a bit sad when everyone goes back to their own room. So when you're choosing somewhere to live, think about whether or not you want to be sociable. Your own space is important too. In the beginning, if you're finding it tough to live with other people, your own space is a haven. It's somewhere where you can relax. In your own room, you can calm down if you're feeling rather 'frazzled', which will make you better company for when you meet up with your flatmates. It also means that you're not always getting under each other's feet.

M And what kind of people is it best to live with?

F Once you've made friends and have been living with them for a while, you'll come to realise that group dynamics are important. There are two options as regards living arrangements: you can live with friends or you can live with strangers. Some people couldn't share a place with someone they don't know. For one thing, you can be more accommodating to people you already know and like. For another, you might not know how much you can trust them. However, moving in with friends comes with a warning. What if you fall out over the washing up? Realising that you could easily destroy a great friendship as housemates, and preparing for that, is one step towards harmony. But you might not want to risk the cost of a friendship and you could decide that living with strangers is the best thing to do. After all, it could be fun, you never know who you might meet. It's just as well to meet up with your new flatmates before you sign anything though. Think about going out with them for the evening. Or at least chat to them while you're looking around the place. Sometimes fate throws you together with people and you get on famously. However, it can be a shock when you have to live with people who you have nothing in common with or who do things that you consider to be anti-social or odd. If you have a choice, try to choose people to live with whose behaviour you think you can bear. If you don't like people playing heavy rock or acid house music all day and night, don't live with them. If you think it's fine to leave dirty socks out in the sitting room, then make sure that you choose people who are similarly untidy. Being considerate is one of the fundamentals to living with other people, but it helps if you have a similar outlook and attitude to life. It's no good if just one of you likes partying all night. Much better that you all do. If you're all into hiking or cycling, you'll understand better that equipment left all over the hall is a fact of life.

Test 4

Track 13   Part 1, p. 90

1

If you don't watch out, you're going to wind up in trouble and don't expect me to get you out of it like I did last time. I know you needed a new suit for your interview, but was it really necessary to spend over a thousand pounds on it, knowing full well the cheque would bounce? I was so embarrassed when the bank manager phoned this morning! What on earth were you thinking of? You don't expect someone to employ you just because you've got a brand name on your back, do you?

2

Lots of people are moving away from the crowded city centres to the countryside and who could blame them? Life in the city has become almost unbearable due to the chaos caused by traffic not to mention the smog. There has also been quite a remarkable increase in respiratory diseases due to people breathing in exhaust fumes while walking or cycling to work and so they've had to opt for the healthier way of life in the countryside. But what about the rest of us who don't earn enough to just hand in our notice and take off? I suppose we'll just have to resort to wearing protective masks when we're out and about!

3

A Did you manage to save anything at all from the flames?
B No, if only we had been warned, we could have got some of our belongings out. But we just stood their in our night clothes and watched while it burned to the ground.
A How awful for you!
B You can say that again, but disaster really struck when I found out we weren't insured!
A What!
B That's right. My husband didn't renew our insurance policy! Apparently, it slipped his mind, and so we've lost everything!

4

The Golden Fleece was the skin of a golden ram which hung in a sacred grove guarded by a dragon. The hero Jason was summoned to win the fleece and he called upon the aid of other Greek heroes. These fifty heroes, including Orpheus and Hercules, were called the Argonauts after the ship they sailed in, the Argo. Upon reaching the land of the fleece, Jason was helped by the king's daughter, Medea, a mighty sorceress. She drugged the dragon, so that she and Jason could escape with the Golden Fleece. The heroes fled in the Argo and sailed along the coast until they got back to Greece.

5

Last Friday, we went on a weekend break to the ancient city of Stratford-upon-Avon. A guide took us on a tour of the city and told us all about the old buildings, historic sites and showed us around some of the houses belonging to the Shakespeare family. In the evening, they had organized a trip to the theatre to see one of Shakespeare's plays which was being put on by the local theatrical group. They were brilliant! My wife and I loved it and will certainly be returning in the not too distant future.

6

I'd been trying to lose weight for ages, when I saw this diet in one of those health magazines and I thought I'd give it a try. All I could eat for the first week was minestrone. Minestrone for lunch and minestrone for dinner and by Saturday lunchtime I just couldn't face another dish of the awful stuff. It didn't make me feel sick or dizzy or anything like that, it just didn't taste particularly appetizing. You can't blame me for throwing in the towel and opting for a nice juicy steak instead. But guess what! When I stood on the scales the next morning I'd lost over 2 kilos!

7

A How do you like your new job then, Steven?
B It's much more rewarding than the last place I worked in. People come to me for advice and I try and help them solve their problems. They might be suffering from backache or they might just want a nice comfy recliner to stretch out on and forget about all their troubles. There's a huge range to choose from and we can get them delivered in no time at all.
A I'll know where to come if my back starts playing up then.
B You bet!

8

I wouldn't go there if I were you. It was just about the worst place I've ever stayed at. When we got there, the room wasn't ready and they made us wait in the reception for ages. Then, when they finally did let us have the key, it wasn't the room we'd asked for. We'd booked a sea-view room and this one looked out over the park! The service in the restaurant was appalling, too and I told them so. I suggested the manager got a better cook unless he wanted all his customers going down with food poisoning!

Track 14   Part 2, p. 91

For thousands of years archaeologists have been trying to solve the puzzle of the origin of Stonehenge and discover a reason why this huge circle of stones was built five thousand years ago to align perfectly on the summer and winter solstice.
For centuries experts have wondered if it was built as a place of worship or if it could have been part of a huge astronomical calendar. Some experts believe it is possible

that the stones were put in place to serve some form of ritual function but despite numerous theories no one really knows why Stonehenge was originally built. A geology team declared that the stones that form the inner ring came from the Preseli Mountains in Wales and had been carried two hundred and forty miles over land and sea. A geomorphologist living in Pembrokeshire contradicted the assumption that the stones had been dug out of a quarry and transported by Bronze Age man to Stonehenge saying that it 'stretched credibility'. It has been suggested in the Oxford Journal of Archaeology that the bluestones were ripped from the ground and moved by glaciers during the ice age. The debate will go on until someone is able to prove beyond doubt what happened one way or the other. The origins of Stonehenge have baffled archaeologists since its discovery in seventeen twenty-three. There are ancient avenues which criss-cross the land surrounding the stones but no one knows what they mean. The most famous of these avenues is the Cursus. This is an extraordinary feature of the landscape stretching for two miles but the reasons why it was built and what it was built for, have not yet been discovered. During a recent excavation on the site, there was a remarkable find. A fragment of an antler which was used as a pick was found while working was being done on an old burial barrow at the end of the Cursus. The archaeologists working on the dig hope to find material which will enable them to possibly date when the burial borrow was built and how it links to the Cursus. There have been many theories over the years. One, that it could have been a racetrack for Roman chariots until it was discovered to be much older than that. A new excavation puts the arrival of the stones at 3000 BC – which is nearly five hundred years earlier than originally thought and suggests that perhaps it was mainly used as a burial site. This conflicts with research that had dated the construction of Stonehenge to 2300 BC and had proposed it was a healing centre. This date was arrived at by carbon dating and was the major find from an excavation inside the henge. It has also been declared that the 2300 BC date relates to the time when the stones were moved from the outer pits to the centre of the site. An earlier theory was that the holes had held bluestones due to a discovery in 1920 in three of the pits of crushed and compacted chalk. The stones were very closely associated with the remains of the dead. Cremation burials were carried out from inside the holes holding the stones and also the areas around them. The archaeologists believe that it is possible that very early in the history of Stonehenge there were fifty-six Welsh bluestones forming one ring which would have measured 87 metres across.
Although Stonehenge has existed for thousands of years, it still holds a fascination not only for archaeologists but also members of the public and the site is visited by up to a million people every year – at the same time Archaeologists and other enthusiasts continue their work in the hope that one day they may find the true reasons for the building of Stonehenge.

Track 15   Part 3, p. 92

1

When we got to the airport we were offered a leaflet giving information about scams involving fake Spanish holiday clubs. It was warning tourists to be wary of touts handing out scratch cards which tell them they have won a prize. Apparently, these cards were being used to lure poor, unsuspecting holiday makers to a high cost sales pitch. Tourists who had attended sales presentations, had ended up spending thousands of pounds in membership fees by signing up for fake holiday clubs. Most of them found they had simply bought access to an internet booking service offering a service which they could have got for free at a travel agent. The leaflet said that, on average, the victims lost about three thousand pounds each with absolutely no hope of getting their money back!

2

Do you remember the good old times when holidays were booked as a package, covering flights, transfers and accommodation and if there were any problems you could usually rely on the travel agent to sort them out? Well, my wife and I decided to try the old-fashioned way and we booked an all-inclusive holiday with 'Holiday World' for our 25th wedding anniversary. Unfortunately, I had a bad fall while on holiday and was advised by the doctor to get in touch with my travel insurance. That's when I discovered from the hotel manager that we had not been booked at the hotel with 'Holiday World' but with 'Comos' – he explained that different parts of our holiday had been booked with different companies. So, we tried to claim through our agent's insurers for the medical costs but because we weren't actually on a package holiday, we weren't able to claim compensation for the accident. Have you ever heard such nonsense?!

3

Two friends of mine booked a package holiday to Sharm-el-Sheikh in Egypt with Corner Street Travel at a cost of £1,438. They'd seen it advertised on TV, so one of them rang up and paid for the whole package, including travel insurance, immediately. A letter confirming full payment arrived, stating they would fly with TVA Airways, but two weeks before the holiday, the airline went into liquidation and they were asked to pay a further £1,000 for new flights. The company they had booked with, had paid separately for flight transfers and accommodation which meant my friends had to rebook their flights and pay the new fare.

They could have claimed a full refund because the airline was covered by insurance, but the travel agency didn't even bother to let them know.

4

There's nothing worse than going on holiday and not being able to get home because the airline has gone into liquidation. A friend of mine is being badly affected. She is due to marry in Florida and has booked all the flights and transfers through a local travel agency. Forty of her guests were due to fly out on 26th September with XL Airlines and all the flights have been cancelled. Poor thing! She was so enthusiastic when she booked. She even paid £3000 in cash because she didn't want to pay the 3% charge on her credit card and now she might have to get a bridging loan so that she can pay for a new set of flights at a later date. She is worried she might not be able to get out there for her own wedding!

5

We had an awful journey to reach our holiday destination in Turkey. Heavy traffic on the motorway in England followed by delays at the airports, not to mention a three and a half hour bus ride to reach the hotel! After sixteen hours travelling, we were both exhausted, so we had a quick snack and retired to bed. The next morning, I awoke to find my sister very excited after waking in the early hours to watch the dawn break and listen to a donkey braying, birds singing and the mosque calling people to prayer. My sister thought this was a fun start to our holiday, whereas I just snuggled further down under the covers and went back to sleep.

Track 16   Part 4, p. 93

Int. In the studio today is musician, James Holland, who's come to tell us about the pleasure and satisfaction that can be gained from the love and practice of music.

Man I could not imagine a life without music, not being able to play an instrument or having access to music whether through radio, television, CDs or concerts. The best thing about music is that anyone can take it up. It is easily accessible and very rewarding, it is also an amazing combination of physical coordination and intellectual and expressive activity.

Int. How would someone with an interest in music go about finding a suitable instrument and learning to play?

Man Well, the first and obvious thing is to decide on the instrument. Most people, whether musical or not, have their favourites. Then, learning to play your chosen instrument, this can be done perhaps with private lessons or depending on your choice of instrument, maybe in a class or with a group of likeminded would be musicians.

Int. What about children? When do you take their wish to learn an instrument and study music seriously?

Man You will soon discover how enthusiastic your child is, by the way they decide on an instrument and whether they practise without always being told to do so. They may find a new way of playing around with their instrument. In other words, they are not just 'practising', but learning to make music with it.

Int. How would you go about helping a child choose an instrument and what age do you think they should start?

Man It needn't be too much of a problem, most children will begin with a piano, recorder, violin or cello, they need to feel comfortable with it. Some instruments are more suitable for younger children: the recorder, for instance, is easy to handle and some stringed instruments are available in smaller versions. Brass and woodwind should be left until they have the strength to blow and they have their second teeth. To find out which type of music your child really likes, you can take them to concerts to listen to live music and find out about different instruments. You shouldn't make the mistake of starting them too young or too soon because lessons can be hard to cope with under the age of eight.

Int. What about children with a disability?

Man Music can be great therapy, it can be a way of exploring the world or simply a pleasurable experience in its own right whether the child is listening to or creating music. Most children respond beautifully to music. Attending music classes is stimulating and it gives the child the chance to socialize with children who don't treat him any differently. One case which comes to mind is David, an autistic boy who ignored his brother for several years. Music therapy has made a positive impact on their lives and their interaction has increased remarkably.

Int. And where can parents find this sort of help if they have a disabled child?

Man If parents are looking for a music therapist, they should contact A.P.M.T, the Association of Professional Music Therapists, as only the therapists who have completed a recognized course are allowed to be state registered. There is also a centre in London called Norway Robins, which provides music therapy, training courses and a research department. It was founded on the belief that we can all respond to music even when ill or disabled. The ability to express ourselves through music and sound is an innate capacity which does not depend on musical skills or verbal language. The children have lots of fun and a great social life as a result of the fact that they play musical instruments. They are learning a universal language beyond words and you don't have to be academic to be musical. So children with differing abilities can play together, this plays an important part in that it can bring together able-bodied and disabled children to enjoy the same musical pastimes.

Test 5

Track 17   Part 1, p. 112

1

Before I came here I worked in sales and really I found the monotony getting to me. Every day was essentially the same. So I took a complete change of direction, retrained and here I am. It's been almost 4 years now and I can honestly say that no day is like the one before. What's particularly rewarding is that I'm helping people who find themselves in difficult situations, due to any number of reasons... health problems, unemployment, to name just two. What's great is that, more often than not I can make some sort of difference to their lives.

2

Well, it was OK I suppose. But to be honest, if you've seen one, you've seen them all. And the final scene was just awful. They're looking up at the stars with far away looks on their faces, when suddenly all these rockets and fireworks start exploding in the sky. He's a tough New York cop and she's an investigative reporter, and at the beginning they hate each other, but you've guessed it, he saves her from a professional killer and it's not long before they're running into each other's arms in a crowded subway station.

3

A So... how was it?

B It wasn't exactly the best two weeks I've ever had. On the first night we went out to a local restaurant and by the time we got back to the hotel Beth was feeling sick and dizzy. The hotel doctor had a look at her and said it was food poisoning.

A How awful!

B It wasn't so bad. It meant that I could just sit around the pool and relax while she was sleeping, instead of dragging me around to see every monument and museum like she usually does.

A You're terrible!

B Don't worry; she got her revenge on the second week. I just wanted to relax but we had to see as much as we could in the time we had left... we ended up shouting at each other in the middle of an ancient convent and then didn't speak until we got home. It's all OK now though. We're both just glad to be back.

4

A There you are. I was beginning to worry.

B Sorry. I was just looking at one of those vases on sale. They're really cheap and I thought it would look good on the TV. And if it didn't I could just bring it back with the receipt and get my money back. But just as I turned it over, the handle came off in my hand. So I just put it down and came back here. I hope nobody noticed me.

A Well, let's just pay for all this stuff and get out of here as soon as we can.

5

All this week in Abbey Road Park you can sample locally made biscuits, cakes and desserts including last year's prize winning carrot cake. Dozens of rides and stalls for all the family as well as music on the main stage from 8. Local band Freddy and the Pacesetters will be performing songs from their new album Phenomenal. Tickets cost 8 pounds for adults, 4 pounds for under 16's.

6

I know, but that's not really that important… she's only my age and hasn't been doing this very long, but management seem to think she's quite capable, and I suppose they must know what they're doing. It's more that with all these cuts she's proposing… most of the junior staff will be out of work and will have to look for other jobs, and who's going to do their share of the work here? You've guessed it… I'll be stuck with it and expected to finish everything on time as always.

7

It seemed like quite a challenge when I heard about the project; I mean playing somebody like Buster Keaton who performed all his own stunts… having to jump from a horse onto a train… it's a bit too much for me, I can't even ride a horse. But after reading the script I was relieved to see that wasn't necessary at all. It's mainly focused on his personal life and so I wouldn't have to face such physical torments. Instead I spent hours every day, for about three months in fact, watching DVDs of his old films, studying his mannerisms and facial expressions. And to be honest with you, I'm more than a little proud of the result.

8

A So I know you're dying to tell me… how's the car?
B To tell you the truth, I'm beginning to think I should have waited a bit longer. I may have made a mistake and rushed into buying it. I just imagined it there in my garage and had to have it.
A Why do you think you've made a mistake?
B It's just that I've spent everything I had on it. I could've just bought something second hand or kept my old one running for another year or so. If I have to take it for repairs any time soon, I don't know how I'll be able to pay for it.

Track 18   Part 2, p.113

The most endangered cat species is the Iberian Lynx, sometimes called the Spanish Lynx. Should this species die out it would be the first feline extinction since the Smilodon, commonly known as the Sabre-Toothed Tiger, 10,000 years ago. Recent studies estimate the number of surviving Iberian lynx to be as few as 100, which is around 400 less than there were in 2000. What does an Iberian Lynx look like? Their leopard-like spots particularly distinguish it from its cousin, the Eurasian Lynx and it is also smaller, with a head and body length between 85 and a 110 centimetres. Males can weigh between 12.9 and 27 kilograms, which is about half the weight of the average Eurasian Lynx. The lynx can live up to a period of thirteen years. The Iberian Lynx's size means that it typically hunts for animals no bigger than rabbits or hares. Rabbits would account for more than 70% of the Lynx's food, but due to Spain's declining rabbit population, the lynx has been forced to attack larger mammals such as young deer or roebuck. The Iberian Lynx hunts alone and follows its prey even up to distances of a 100 kilometres. Or it lies in wait for its prey for many hours. It uses the four sets of whiskers on its ears and chin to sense its victim. They are active at night. They stay active in winter and their fur becomes thicker and paler. In extreme weather, they take shelter in caves or trees. The Iberian Lynx was once widespread all over the peninsula but it is now restricted to very small areas, mainly mountainous areas covered with vegetation. Its drastic decline over recent decades is due to loss of habitat, reduction in prey and high non-natural mortality from road kills, predator control and hunting, although it is under legal protection and it is no longer legal to hunt them. It was recently thought that the only breeding Iberian lynxes were in the Doñana National Park in Andalucía, southern Spain, but in 2007 a previously unknown population was discovered in Castilla-La Mancha in central Spain. In March 2005, for the first time Iberian Lynxes managed to breed in captivity. 3 healthy cubs were born at a breeding centre in Doñana. In 2009 it was announced that 3 more cubs had been born in the same centre. Typically a mother will give birth to 3 cubs after a gestation period of 60 days. Iberian Lynx conservation is now under way through political campaigning and lobbying from individuals and organizations such as SOS Lynx. Important progress has been made in a number of ways. The foundation of the breeding programme in Andalucía, prevention of further construction in areas the Iberian lynx lives, and the halting of proposals for new roads in problematic areas, such as the new motorway that had been planned between Ciudad Real in La Mancha and Cordoba in Andalucía. Despite these successes, challenges and conflicting pressures remain. The World Wildlife Foundation has been urging Spanish authorities for over two years to close a road which crosses the Doñana national park, as Callum Rankine of the WWF says, 'With such a small population, the accidental loss of just one individual on the road brings the species closer to the brink of extinction.'

Track 19   Part 3, p. 114

1

It came as a complete surprise. Right out of the blue she came home and told me she'd been made redundant from work and said why didn't we just take off for a year and travel around the world. Well, it just all seemed to make sense. I wasn't enjoying my work at the time and was thinking about doing something else. Her company had given her quite a generous redundancy package and also we could rent out our house for the year; that would give us enough to live on for the year as long as we were careful with our money. And I'm pleased to say that we were, apart from the occasional few luxuries here and there… you know, meals in expensive restaurants for special occasions like birthdays or anniversaries, that kind of thing.

2

It's something I'd been looking into for some time. To tell you the truth, it's something I've wanted to do ever since I was a kid. It just never seemed that it would be something I could realistically do, so it just remained a dream. But after somebody told me how cheap it was when you actually got there, I started to do some serious research. And really, although actually getting there is very expensive, the price of the hotels, restaurants and travelling around the country is so low compared to places in Europe, it means that in total you're not paying much more than you would for a cheap holiday on the beach in Greece or Spain. And it's a lot more interesting than just lying around on a beach somewhere. It was great. I'm going back there next year. I didn't think I would ever be able to say that.

3

It's not every day you go on honeymoon, but if you ask me it was all a bit over the top. We had our own private beach and the staff couldn't do enough for us; they wouldn't let us do a thing for ourselves. For example if I tried to pour myself a drink, somebody would suddenly appear and take the bottle out of my hand and finish pouring it. I know it's all these luxuries that you're paying for but it's a bit much for me and wasn't something I was comfortable with. I suppose you must just get used to it after a while, but all the time I kept thinking that it would have been a better idea if we'd used that money to buy a washing machine and some new furniture instead of going to all that expense.

4

To tell you the truth, the hotel was a bit of a letdown. The pictures in the brochure were flattering to say the very least. The restaurant was supposed to be five star but I can honestly say I've had better food in a motorway service station. It wasn't all bad though, the area itself was lovely. The beach near the village was lovely and had everything you could ask for… clean white sand, beautiful blue sea, palm trees. And the locals were really friendly and really made a fuss of the kids. I think we'll go back there soon, but we'll definitely stay in a different hotel, that one wasn't good value for money at all.

5

I'd really been looking forward to going there and I wasn't disappointed. Not in the least. From the moment you arrive there you feel immersed in its history. It's the birthplace of civilisation after all, and every street you walk down reminds you of this. I know some people wouldn't find it much fun, to be going from boring museum to boring museum, but it wasn't like that. When you see some of the collections they have in the museums, and you see it in context to the city itself, well, it's an extraordinary feeling. The weather wasn't great but I don't think that spoiled it for us at all. It's not like you go to a place like that just to sit on the beach and get a tan. We had a week there, but really you'd need a month just to see everything.

Track 20   Part 4, p. 115

Int. It's been described as the fastest ball game in the world, and is played in places as far away as Australia and South Africa but it actually comes from our western neighbours over in Ireland. Many of us know next to nothing about this sport so it will come as a surprise to learn that it has been played competitively all over our country since the 19th century. Sean McGinn of the British Gaelic Athletic Association is here to tell us a bit about the sport of hurling. Hi, Sean, thanks for coming. Could you give us a brief description of hurling?

Sean Sure. Well, it's played on a pitch of around 140 metres long and 85 metres wide, although for youth matches it's considerably smaller. There are two teams of 15 people and each player has a slim bat called a hurley which is made from ash wood. Players use the hurley to propel a small leather ball, which is slightly bigger than a tennis ball. There are two ways to score points during a match – by scoring into the goal and past the goalkeeper, whose hurley is slightly bigger than the outfield players'… just to give him a chance… or you can score by hitting the ball over the bar but between two long posts. A goal scored past the goalkeeper is worth 3 points while putting it over the bar is worth 1.

Int. Well that all sounds relatively easy. Is it?

Sean Not so easy as all that I'm afraid. As you said earlier, it is the fastest ball game in the world. A good hurler can hit the ball up to 150 kilometres an hour and the ball can travel as much as 110 metres. There are also a few rules that make the whole thing trickier for the players. You can't just pick up the ball from the floor, you have to flick it up using the hurley. You can't carry the ball in your hand for more than 4 steps, so you have to run while balancing the ball on the hurley, which is no easy thing. There are also restrictions on the way you can tackle another player, so all in all it's a sport that requires a high level of skill and years of practice.

Int. And tell us how popular the sport is outside Ireland.

Sean Well the history of Ireland is dominated by emigration. While the country itself has a population of less than 7 million, it's often claimed that there are over 70 million people around the world with Irish ancestry. Nearly 11% of Americans see themselves as Irish-Americans. My own parents came over to Britain from Galway in the West of Ireland in the 1930s. Wherever these emigrants went, they took their sport with them. So now hurling is played in places such as Britain, the USA, Canada, Argentina, Australia, New Zealand, South Africa, as well as places in continental Europe – for example there are teams from Brussels, from Luxembourg, from Munich, Paris and Zurich.

Int. And what would you say the appeal of the sport is?

Sean As well as the cultural aspect: keeping in touch with your roots, the game itself is so fast moving and so skilful that it's hard to take your eyes away from the action for even a second. Also in these days of the commercialisation of sport when you have footballers or formula one drivers earning more in a week than most of us will see in a lifetime, it's important to remember that even at the very highest level, hurling players are amateurs. That and the absence of violence between supporters…even in the most important matches there's no segregation between rival fans… gives the sport a purity and nobility that I don't think you get in other sports.

Int. Thanks, Sean. I think we all know a little more about what sounds like a fascinating sport. That was Sean McGinn of the British Gaelic Athletic Association talking about the sport of hurling.

Test 6

Track 21 Part 1, p. 134

1

I don't know what's got into him. He used to be such a sweet boy. He'd come round to the house at Christmas time and sing such lovely carols. My husband used to take him fishing on Sunday mornings… if you could get him out of bed on time of course. Now he hardly says a word to either of us and he's been getting into terrible trouble in the classroom. The headmaster has asked them all to come in for a meeting. We're all worried he's going to be expelled from school.

2

In the end I just decided it wasn't really what I was looking for. Sure, if you compare it to places in the centre of town, it certainly wasn't bad value for money. But, at the end of the day, it's just me, no wife, no kids, why would I need two extra bedrooms? I know it's more expensive to stay here in town, but I don't really want to spend an hour or more commuting from the outskirts rather than just walking half an hour to work.

3

All my friends laughed when I told them I'd bought tickets. 'How old are you?' they asked, and I suppose they've got a point – I think the lead singer is only a couple of years younger than my granddad. But I've always loved their music… well…their early stuff from the 60s and 70s… that's why I felt really let down when they spent 40 minutes playing songs from their new album, which I have to say, isn't great. But once that was out of the way they went on to play just

about every song they've ever written. You've got to admire their energy… I can't imagine my granddad running around on stage for that long.

4

I've been there before, I went there with my wife to celebrate our third anniversary, which was five years ago now. We had a great time just sitting around in the squares, getting a tan and seeing the sights. I don't imagine I'll get to see many sights this time, unless you count a hotel room, the inside of a taxi and a conference centre as sights. Luckily it's only 4 days and I'll be back on Saturday… I'd better be, my brother's getting married and I'm the best man!

5

Pres. So Brian, this is it… here comes the final question. Let me remind you, you've used all three life lines and if you choose to play and get the answer wrong you'll walk home with nothing. If, after hearing the question, you decide not to play, you keep the two thousand pounds you've already won. But… if you get the answer right… you win the jackpot of ten thousand pounds. OK? Here it is… who won the European Football Cup in 1979 and 1980? Was it A: Real Madrid, B: Liverpool or C: Nottingham Forest

Brian Well… I think it was Nottingham Forest but I'm not absolutely sure… so I think I'll keep what I've already won. I've had a lovely day, thanks for everything.

Pres. Well, Brian, you're a cautious man… and you were right… it was answer C: Nottingham Forest. A round of applause everybody for Brian Smith, a worthy winner.

6

A Hello Scottish Rail, how can I help you?

B Hi, I'd like to buy a return ticket to Glasgow please.

A When were you thinking of travelling back?

B I'm not exactly sure, maybe next Monday but it's not really definite.

A Well, an open return is £67.20 which means you can come back any time before the end of next month. If you decide to buy a fixed return for next Monday that's £43.50. But you know, a single is £25… so if you buy a single and then another single when you decide to come back, you're only spending £6.50 more than the fixed return.

B Ah… that's what I'll do then. Can I have one of those please.

A Sure. That's £25 please.

7

I've been really surprised by their reaction to be honest. They've been really supportive, Dad even lent me the money for the deposit and helped me move all my stuff in. That's the odd thing, they have such an old fashioned attitude I thought that never in a million years would they let me. I think that's what made me decide to leave really, we never seemed to see eye to eye on anything and would get on each other's nerves and row about almost everything.

My new place is a little nearer to the office, but only about another 10 minutes on the bus. What's great is that now I have my own space and I can just invite a friend round, cook dinner, watch a DVD, that sort of thing, without having to check with mum and dad if it's OK… and possibly having a blazing row about it.

8

Wellco Supermarkets are offering another sensational summer savings sizzler. In our East Park, Church Street and North Road branches, buy 2 one and a half litre bottles of premiocola for just £1.40, that's a saving of nearly 50%… and that's not all. Collect the tokens on each bottle top and for every 6 you'll get a free margherita or tex mex pizza at PizzaNation in the high street. Enter our free draw to win a holiday for two in Punta Cana, Mexico when you spend over £25 on any Wellco own-brand products.

Track 22 Part 2, p. 135

Douglas Finch is to be awarded the Honorary Degree of Doctor of Business Administration in recognition of his outstanding scientific, design, and entrepreneurial achievements and their important contribution to the history and reputation of Bristol. Douglas Finch was born near Glasgow and attended Allan Glen's School before reading aeronautical engineering at Glasgow University, from which he graduated in 1961. He gained a Master's Degree in Industrial Engineering at Cornell University, USA in 1963 before returning to the United Kingdom and joining the Bristol Aeroplane Company.

He joined the Bristol Gliding Club and in 1965 received the Silver 'C' Gliding Badge. In

1967 he helped build the 'Bristol Belle', a red and white striped balloon which made its first flights at Weston-on-the-Green near Oxford. It was the first modern hot air balloon in Western Europe. In 1968 Doug Finch was issued with the first ever Private Pilot's Licence for Hot Air Balloons.

The success of Doug Finch in translating his ballooning expertise into a commercial concern is reflected in the birth and success of his company, Finch Balloons of Bristol, which was formed by Finch in 1971 – five years after he constructed his first balloon. The new company was based in Dutton, Bristol, where a total of twenty-nine balloons were made in the basement of the property. 1971 also saw Finch build Golden Falcon, a balloon designed specifically to fly across the Sahara.

In 1972 Doug Finch received the Royal Aeronautical Club Bronze Medal, the first awarded for hot air airships. A year later he was awarded the Royal Aeronautical Club Silver Medal for the first balloon flight over the Alps. In the same year he received the Lighter Than Air Society (USA) Achievement Award for the development of the first hot air ship. Five years later he attempted the first Atlantic crossing by balloon for which he received the Royal Aeronautical Club Gold Medal. In 1978 his attempt to make the premier Atlantic crossing by balloon ended when bad weather forced his heated helium balloon 'Zanussi' down after a 2,000 mile flight from Canada.

The Finch company moved to its present site in Gellingborough in 1983 and in the following years all of the records for distance and duration were taken by pilots flying Finch balloons. In 1989 Finch Balloons Limited received the Queen's Award for Export, confirmation that Doug Finch had made Bristol the undisputed balloon manufacturing capital of the world. During the 1990s interest in becoming the first to fly around the world by balloon became intense and almost all the contenders have used Finch helium/hot air balloons.

Doug Finch has advanced the science, technology and art of balloon flight to the highest level. His factory in Bristol is the world's largest and last year he was awarded the Prince Philip Design Award. Doug Finch will receive his Honorary Degree of Doctor of Business Administration at the award ceremony at Bristol Business School.

Track 23 Part 3, p. 136

1

People tell me I should cash in on it, sell up and move out to the country. Prices have gone up so much around here that I could get a lovely place somewhere rural. I don't know though, it had never really occurred to me before. I've lived half my life here and don't really see much reason for a change. But while you might say the area has gone up-market and improved, with these new bistros and shops, well it's lost something too. A lot of the character it used to have… I mean, now I don't even know my neighbours' names and they don't know mine. So I'm not sure if I should stick around now. Moving… well, it's food for thought.

2

There was a time around here that you could leave your front door open morning, noon and night. Kids just played in the street unsupervised and only came home when it got dark or their dinner was on the table. Everybody knew everybody else…and their business… so it wasn't all great! … But over the last few years it's got worse and worse and I've no idea why, I really don't. Mrs Peters at number 36, she was mugged just last Thursday, 50 pounds and her mobile phone she lost.

3

When we saw it we just fell in love with it. The old wooden floors, the heavy oak doors, the delightful bay windows… and the garden… the garden's going to be glorious in spring. We'll have picnics, maybe even barbecues. Of course there's lots of work to be done before it's perfect, if it ever will be… But we seem to be settling in. Most of the local shopkeepers seem to know our names now and most people say hello in the street. It's such a change from living in the city. And when the kids go back to school there's a really good one at the other end of the village. I'll probably have to walk them there though… the high street is very busy with cars and I don't want to risk them crossing a busy road on their own.

4

Well, with the kids now, there's just not enough room for all of us. We had to do it really. Obviously, I would have liked to have stayed here, but it's for the best. It was just impractical really. And now we'll have a lovely place. I've lived here since I left home. I never imagined then how much my life would change. Look out of the window, see that shop, that's where I bought my first suit for my first day of work, and there's the café where I met Karen, my wife. The idea of moving was hard at first, leaving all these memories behind. Still, it's for the best and it's not like we're moving to the other side of the world. It's only a ten minute drive and I can pop back whenever I like.

5

I realise now it wasn't the right thing to do. We jumped in too quick; we just took one look at the cottage and the village and we fell in love. We didn't really think about the practicalities. It all seemed so idyllic really. Country houses with beautiful gardens, cricket on the village green, the village fete, the duck pond… it seemed like we were going back in time. But once you're used to all that, spent a year or so here… well…that's when the realities kick in. There's not really much to do. If we want to go to the cinema it's a half hour drive to the multiplex on the ring road. If we want to eat in a good restaurant or see an exhibition we have to go into town, which with traffic can take over an hour and a half. And while the kids don't mind it now, I dread to think what they'll be like when they're a bit older… there's literally nothing for teenagers to do here. I guess we should have given it a bit more practical thought before we dived in and moved.

Track 24 Part 4, p. 137

Int. We've all heard of fun-runs and half marathons, maybe we've even competed in them… but how many of us have heard of ultra-marathons? My guest today is Stan Woodcock who is going to tell us all about ultra-marathons. Hi, Stan, thanks for coming. Maybe I could start by asking you the obvious question… what exactly is an ultra-marathon?

Stan Hello Roy, thanks for inviting me onto the programme. Well, you know there's no straightforward answer to your question. Not all ultra-marathons are the same. The simplest answer I can give you is that it involves running further than a normal marathon, which is 42.195 kilometres. Basically you could divide them into two types as well, those that cover a specific distance and those that take place within a specific time period, with the winner being the runner who has covered the most distance.

Int. What sort of distances and time periods are we talking about here?

Stan Well, the timed events range from 6, 12 and 24 hours to 3 and 6 days. In terms of the distance races, the most common distances are 50 and 100 kilometres.

Int. Six days? Surely here in Britain, we'd run out of anywhere to run to!

Stan No – timed events are generally run on a track or a short road course, usually about a kilometre in length.

Int. And how popular are ultra-marathons?

Stan More popular than you'd think. In Europe alone there were more than 200 ultra-marathons last year. There are a few in Africa, including the world's oldest, the 89 kilometre 'comrades marathon' in South Africa which attracts about 12,000 runners a year and a 250 kilometre race in Namibia called 'racing the planet'… it's becoming more popular in Asia. Taiwan, Japan and Korea have all hosted ultra-marathons, and India held its first in Bangalore in 2007. There's even an ultra-marathon held in Antarctica!

Int. And I believe you've just returned from the United States; tell us about that. From what you told me before the programme, it sounds impossible!

Stan Well, I took part in the Badwater Ultra-marathon. Which is a terrific test of your personal endurance. It's a 215 km course which starts at 85 metres below sea level and ends at the top of Mount Whitney in Death Valley, California… 2,548 metres above sea level. What makes it particularly tricky is that it's held in July, when temperatures can reach 49 degrees in the shade. A guy called Al Arnold pioneered the course, first attempting it in 1974, but he failed to finish due to dehydration. He tried again the following year but sustained a knee injury, but in 1977 he was the first to finish it, with a time of eighty hours.

Int. That sounds like quite a trial, Stan. Can I ask you just one last question, and I hope it doesn't sound rude… but, why do you do it? It sounds crazy!

Stan Don't worry, I'm asked that all the time. Maybe I used to ask myself too. But I can tell you this… it has taught me how I can take responsibility for my life and thereby guide my own destiny instead of blaming other people and being victimised by my own imperfections. It confirmed that the anger and rage that exists in most of us is based on our inability to accept our own inadequacies. It has taught me that we all have the strength and conviction to deal with adversity – if we can just tap into it. But more than anything, it has left me feeling profoundly grateful for my family and friends, appreciation of what I have, who I am, and where I am going in my life.

Int. Stan Woodcock, thanks for coming in and speaking to us.